ARCHITECTURE IN DETAIL

Chicago

ARCHITECTURE IN DETAIL

Chicago

Thomas J. O'Gorman

PRC

For Mary O'Connor Curran

I am deeply grateful to the following for their assistance in view-ing and photographing Chicago's most remarkable architectural wonders: The photographs of Simon Clay display the spirit of Chicago architecture at its best. He is a grand chap with which to work. Kevin Lennon, Jeff Reiter, John Buck, Dan McCaffrey, Drew Neiman, Commissioner Mary Dempsey, Margot Burke Holland and the staff of the Chicago Public Library, Karen Skubish and the staff of the Newberry Library, Reverend Daniel Mayall, Most Reverend Timothy J. Lyne and the staff of Holy Name Cathedral, Jim Soring, Ethel Zitnik, Kayla Ehrlich, Christopher G. Kennedy, Joanna Mannino, Jennifer L. Newton, Ann Donnell, Betsy Traczek, Pat Cahill, Sue Draths, Richard Solomon, and Mark Steinke all treasure good architecture and made important contributions to this work.

Page 1: The squat features of the Merchandise Mart become optically altered when reflected in the curving green glass planes of the 333 West Wacker Building designed by Kohn Pedersen Fox (1983).
Page 2: The Chicago Board of Trade shimmers in the golden glow of evening illumination in LaSalle Street.

Photo acknowledgments:

The publisher wishes to thank Simon Clay for taking all the photography in this book, and Thomas J. O'Gorman for his help in arranging the photo shoot. Additional thanks to all those who kindly gave their permission for photography to be taken on their premises. With the exception of the images listed below, all photography is copyright © Chrysalis Images: Page 22 and 23: supplied by Daniel Newman; Page 47: © Joseph Sohm; ChromoSohm Inc./CORBIS; Page 62: © Robert Holmes/COR-BIS; Page 63: © Sandy Felsenthal/CORBIS; Pages 70 and 76: © G.E. Kidder Smith/CORBIS. The front cover shows: the towers of Marina City (© Chrysalis Images) and the back cover shows: the Harold Washington Library (© Chrysalis Images).

Produced 2003 by
PRC Publishing Ltd,
64 Brewery Road, London N7 9NT
A member of Chrysalis Books plc

This edition published 2003
Distributed in the U.S. and Canada by:
Sterling Publishing Co., Inc.
387 Park Avenue South
New York, NY 10016

© 2003 PRC Publishing Ltd

ISBN 1 85648 668 0

Printed and bound in Malaysia

Contents

Introduction

Wonderful and terrible is God's Chicago. It lies beside Lake Michigan like the Leviathan in the Book of Job. 'I will not conceal his parts, nor his power, nor his comely proportions.'

Sir Shane Leslie

Chicago has architecture in its blood. The contours and shapes of local living have always been enriched by a special attitude toward architectural design that is bold, inventive, sophisticated, and modern. Architecture here enjoys a unique primacy of place unrivaled anywhere else in the nation. The images of Chicago architecture are familiar around the world, its edgy, progressive artistry setting a new standard in fresh urban design.

Since the 1880s, architecture in Chicago has been robustly evolving through the epic work of some of the world's most distinguished and revolutionary architects, most of them homegrown. In Chicago they still enjoy larger-than-life reputations and their names are known and celebrated throughout the city. The panache of Chicago architecture is not just the provenance of the elite. Instead, it is a real feature of everyday life. Strong opinions about architecture are freely expressed with the same emotions normally reserved for the city's two professional baseball teams or the quality of deep-dish pizza. It is as much a part of the local landscape as the waters of Lake Michigan or a ride round the Loop on the "L."

Architecture has injected its way into the very vocabulary of the city. Certain phrases common in Chicago living help to explain the temper and character of Chicago and its people.

Right: The 365-foot green glass façade of the 333 West Wacker Drive Building by Kohn Pedersen Fox (1983). The building's shape is said to follow the curve of the Chicago River.

"Make no little plans..." one maxim announces as both a challenge and a warning. "Form follows function," another points out with a hard eye to practical reason. "Less is more," still another urges, validating the shared ethos of common simplicity that deepens both beauty and strength.

What makes these sayings so rich and useful for contemporary Chicagoans is not that they were spoken by some local divines as an entreaty to their congregation, but that they are the words of Chicago architects whose impact remains firmly in people's minds, many years after their passing. Their words of reason are as much about how life should be lived, as they are about how to fashion public spaces or private homes. The first saying, by Daniel Burnham, lingers as a lasting philosophical legacy which is still pertinent to people of spirit. The second, by Louis Sullivan, demonstrates a rational practicality that is essential in Chicago. The last, from Ludwig Mies van der Rohe, is an invitation to modernity, a journey which is made easier without the clutter of excess. Chicago architects really do inhabit a pantheon of local nobility which, at the same time, goes hand in hand with everyday lives.

Chicago has been an inventive place from its beginning. Incorporated as a city in 1837, its unparalleled urban explosion was fueled by vast commercial and industrial success—an outgrowth of its enviable geographic location, as much as its pioneer inventiveness. In 1848, the linking of Lake Michigan to the Illinois River by the construction of the I&M Canal connected the city to all the inland waterways of the nation. By 1860, it was the railroad hub of the nation. Its centrality at the very heart of the nation gave it an unusual commercial transportation leverage. Huge fortunes were there to be made.

History and geography created Chicagoans' taste for architecture of both purpose and refinement. The Great Fire of 1871 laid waste to three-fifths of the original city. More than 17,000 buildings perished in the central business district alone. In the

Left: Alfred S. Alschuler's 1923 classical Greek Revival commercial high-rise—the twenty-two-story London Guarantee Trust.

Right: The gray stone cladding and green recessed windows of the Leo Burnett Building.

aftermath, many saw it as a blessing in disguise. The poet Vachel Lindsay summed up that sentiment when he noted, "The Chicago Fire should occur many times. Each successive time the buildings rise smarter, less expensive, more economical, more beautiful...America needs to be gone all over again." In an instant, the fire erased the unplanned, disorganized chaos that was the first Chicago. On the clean slate of the smoldering prairie, a "Second City" rose and made itself the talk of the nation. Charles Patrick Keeley's Prairie-Gothic Holy Name Cathedral (1874) stands as a symbol of that starting over. So outstanding was the rebuilding of Chicago, it was said to be both a miracle and a mystery.

Chicago has always been a place for inventive people. That inventiveness was a magnet to a steady stream of transplanted New Englanders who found in Chicago a freedom from the con-strictions of Yankee living. Immigrants also found the city a welcome place to begin again. The rapid flow of foreign labor to Chicago galvanized its rebirth and economic success. There was room to settle and open space in which to reinvent oneself. The city's dusty frontier character dissolved in its fast-paced progress. A burgeoning civility became the catalyst for new refine-ments, including the taste for new and inventive architecture. It is no accident that the world's first skyscraper made its debut in Chicago in 1885 when William LeBaron Jenny used steel-frame fabrication to assemble his ten-story Home Insurance Building on LaSalle Street.

Jenny's high-rise became the wonder of the age and went on to inspire an entire generation of young Chicago architects whose influence continues today. Their work shaped the landscape and commerce of the city, earning them the distinction of creating the first "Chicago School" of

architectural design. Jenny's disciples—Daniel Burnham, Louis Sullivan, Martin Roche, and William Holabird—altered the architectural texture of Chicago and the nation. Their genius endures, like the dramatic artistry and utility of the buildings they created and that still function in the everyday life of Chicago.

Creative architectural partnerships were established in Chicago that blended a timeless artistic ability with advancing technological skills. The result was that well before the turn of the century buildings of remarkable beauty rose higher and higher, incorporating this dual dimension of Chicago style. When Louis Sullivan and Dankmar Adler collaborated on their first major commission, the Auditorium Building and Theater, they sent all Chicagoans reeling in 1889 with their breathtaking eighteen-story hotel, theater, and office complex, the first of its kind. The building was detailed in an organic elegance, but it was also cerebral in its exceptional application of expansive engineering—the Auditorium was the first building to be air-conditioned. No structure in the city had ever soared so high and its tower with observation deck was the highest point in the city. Architecture transported Chicagoans into another age by redefining what the city could become. Chicago architecture was not only utilitarian, it was aesthetic and spiritual. Sullivan and Adler unleashed a dynamic force within the tradition of Chicago living—architecture so substantial and dramatic that it echoed the city's vibrant perception of itself.

The partnership of Daniel Burnham and John Wellborn Root was also deeply influential in reshaping the aesthetics of Chicagoans. With their Rookery Building (1888) on LaSalle Street they revolutionized interior commercial utility, while dazzling everyone with their industrial artistic

Left: The black anodized aluminum crossbeam braces of the tapered 100-story John Hancock Building on Michigan Avenue.

Right: The lobby interior of the Leo Burnett Building is fashioned of Rosa Portugala marble and pine-green African granite.

flair. At their Reliance Building (1895) on State Street, their inspired efforts forged the prototype of the glass-and-steel-framed high-rise from which every glass and steel box in America descends. Such influence marked the Chicago way.

Chicago architecture created an energy which catapulted the city to the forefront of the nation. Such successful architecture created not only a community of invigorated disciples, but also a wide array of interested clients. Chicago was an important city of business. Its location in the heartland placed it in perfect proximity to the bountiful sources of argri-business. Its important transportation business, shaped by the power of the railroads, provided the city with plenty of muscled industrial and commercial barons who saw architecture as the perfect way of adding image to their enterprise.

Chicago architecture was not merely the expression of an intellectual or philosophical aesthetic, but it also had commercial viability. The power of business was behind it. Soaring architecture, tastefully embellished, appealed to the daring of the city's leading commercial titans. As Chicago's fortunes rose, so did the opportunities for the expansion of Chicago's architecture of substance. It was visibly altering the shape and character of the city with an organized sense of development that reflected its urban strength and intensity. In the Monadnock Building (1889), not only Burnham and Root, but also Holabird and Roche, unleashed a *tour de force* executing an epic Midwestern design. Architecture provided more than shelter and space, it layered the urban grid with a rich sense of purpose and pride.

Chicago fortunes bankrolled the work of America's most distinguished architects. They reshaped the city vertically and horizontally. Chicago architects at the turn of the century were sensitive to the necessity of providing clients with designs they understood and appreciated, but they were also aware of the emerging styles that distinguished their work from the rest of the nation. Midwestern pragmatism and Prairie utility gave birth to an architectural expression that was pure Chicago. Richard E. Schmidt, Hugh M.G. Garden, and others expressed a restraint in ornamental embellishment and a crisp geometric polish in their design that continued the traditions of the Chicago School. At the Madelener House (1902), they blended the ethos of the Chicago School with vestiges of Louis Sullivan, their mentor, and Frank Lloyd Wright. Domestic architecture was raised to a new artistry by the adherents of the Chicago School's refined self-control. In the process, they were imbued with the spirit of a deepening modern aesthetic that would eventually become emblematic of the city's urbane identity.

Opportunities to produce buildings of growing magnitude and historic artistry expanded during the 1920s, an era of unparalleled prosperity and development in Chicago. Some of the most significant structures in the city's skyline were created during this time. Economic prosperity and urban development widened the footprint of high-rise construction. No area of the city became more visibly transformed during this period than the land along the banks of the Chicago River

near Michigan Avenue. The Wrigley Building (1921), the Tribune Tower (1925), the Jewelers Building (1926), and the Merchandise Mart (1930) stretched the commercial life of the city, as well as its level of high architectural sophistication. It also marked the growing influence of a new group of Chicago architects who were the heirs to the architectural legacy of Burnham, Root, Sullivan, and Roche. Graham, Anderson, Probst, and White assumed the mantle of this legacy. Their work displayed a grandeur reflective of both Chicago and the age.

Left: The Rookery Building, Burnham and Root's masterpiece of inventive Chicago prairie design.

Above Right: The elevator banks of the Leo Burnett Building and the polished stainless steel and amber-glass light fixtures.

Classical designs, imbued with the Art Deco tastes of the 1920s, filled the commercial heart of the city with an unforgettable elegance and sweeping architectural style. They doubled the height of the city when they pushed new, monster-size structures like the LaSalle National Bank (1934) to completion. This challenged not only the laws of aerodynamics and physics, but also local aesthetics, with a masterpiece defined by an unusual simplicity and featuring no external ornamentation. At the Chicago Board of Trade, the new partnership of John Holabird and John Wellborn Root, Jr., each a son of a Chicago architectural giant, created a timeless symbol to Chicago commerce and the most stirring structure in the financial district. As the city joined the nation and the world in the Great Depression and the ensuing World War, architecture and high-rise development in Chicago was stilled, until the advent of its most dramatic expression came in the post-war era.

The lid blew off a simmering architectural kettle in Chicago in the late 1940s as a new age in its urban architecture came into being with Mies van der Rohe and the proponents of the International Style of minimalist design. A "second" Chicago School came into being that reconfigured the tastes and skyline of the city. In utter simplicity, Mies's lakefront "glass box" apartment complex (1949) challenged everything most Chicagoans understood about architectural design. When the local architectural firm of Skidmore, Owings, and Merrill added the new headquarters of Inland Steel (1958) to the downtown cityscape, a structure that reflected Miesian minimal design, Chicago not only received its first new commercial high-rise since the Great Depression, it also entered into an architectural revolution that would change the concept of how people lived and worked. Less became more and more and more.

The new minimalism expressed an important aesthetic of the post-war world—a vibrant sense of freedom and openness to change. As science and technology made extraordinary advances in everyday living, the glass and steel simplicity of modernism seemed appropriate and expressive of the transitions that were unfolding everywhere. As Chicago's business community awoke from its long nap, modernism in architectural design offered an economical and uncluttered style for new developments. Miesian black steel and glass minimalism became a Chicago signature and an intimate part of the city's bold initiatives in the 1960s. Mies' sprawling Federal Complex (1964), five buildings that form the expansive offices, courtrooms, and post office facilities of the U.S. government, altered the cityscape with an explosive burst of energy.

Skidmore, Owings, and Merrill became a leader in the movement to minimalism. Their refined and imaginative architectural expression joined Mies in redefining Chicago architecture in the modern age. In structures like their Equitable Building (1965), they introduced Chicago minimalism to Michigan Avenue, beside the venerable Tribune Tower and the Wrigley Building, defining a new age of eclecticism. The partnership of Bruce Graham and Fazlur Kahn brought Skidmore world attention with their soaring accomplishment of the John Hancock Center (1969) and the Sears Tower (1974), the world's tallest building. Demonstrating a dramatic capacity for highly complex engineering and singular slender designs, Graham and Kahn tantalized Chicagoans by their capacity to build to unprecedented heights and delighted them with the notoriety of the world. Minimalism has gone on to become an abundant design concept in Chicago that moves across its streets, framing its urban character with a restrained dignity and strength.

Chicago's reverence for the wide historical perspective that its architecture displays is reinforced by the addition of postmodern design. The familiar historic architectural expressions that are often exaggerated in this style became a part of the skyline in the 1980s and 1990s. At the James R. Thompson Center (1985), Helmut Jahn, Chicago's "bad-boy" of architecture, plays with a blend of styles, both modern and historic, in creating his capitol "dome" that serves as the seat of Illinois government in Chicago. The subtle political irony of the structure must be studied. Historic expression is even more dramatic in Thomas Beeby's Harold Washington Library (1992) that is a massive Romanesque titan sprinkled with whimsy. Postmodernism here is enjoyable, but a jolt to local tastes with almost five decades of minimalism under their belts.

Fresh and exciting modern designs continue to massage Chicagoans' taste for grand buildings of remarkable utility. Since the start of the twenty-first century, only one great commercial high-rise has been completed, though more are underway. The UBS Tower (2001) represents the beginning of a new era in high-tech commercial design that is both well proportioned and elegant. Chicago's powerful local economy continues to drive a steam engine of architectural splendor, while the city enjoys an unprecedented renaissance in domestic residential expansion at the city center. A new urban landscape is being fashioned by this expanding population. The urban infrastructure is expanding to accommodate the growing numbers of new city dwellers as well creating an even more vibrant and handsome architectural terrain. Frank Geary's lakefront music pavilion (2003), currently under construction, is the talk of the town for its edgy, exploding style of structural design.

The buildings that have been selected for this book have been chosen because of their importance in the everyday life of Chicago. Their singular architectural continuity, beauty, utility, and place in local tradition make each of them important to city life. Their history and the role they have played in the lives of Chicagoans also makes them worthy of your attention. Together, these twenty buildings combine to tell the expansive tale of Chicago's unique architectural contribution to the evolution of modern design. But first and foremost these buildings are alive in the comings and goings of real human beings. Many of them have stood the test of time and survive as fresh and exciting as the day they were built. Others have made an extraordinary contribution, not only to Chicago life, but also to the life of American architecture. This work will provide you with an understanding of why Chicagoans have such an expansive appreciation for the size, shape, style, and sophistication of the buildings that they call home. They are expressive of a singular American character and the brawny Prairie Style.

Right: Stainless steel and green marble in the south lobby of the 333 West Wacker Building.

Holy Name Cathedral

Architect: Patrick Charles Keeley

Built: 1874

The Roman Catholic Cathedral of the Archdiocese of Chicago, known as Holy Name, rose like much of the city from the ashes of the Great Fire of 1871. Designed and built by architect Patrick Charles Keeley, the new cathedral opened in 1874 as a proud neo-gothic structure formed from true yellow Illinois limestone. It is the same material used to build the famed Chicago Water Tower, just two blocks east, the only public structure to survive the ravages of the fire. The cathedral still bears the imprint of one of Chicago's more sinister eras. It is said markings in the cornerstone were made by bullets in the 1920s when bootlegger Dion O'Banyon, who occupied a florist shop across the street from the cathedral, was gunned down by rival mobsters.

Holy Name Cathedral was built in a quiet, refined urban neighborhood, just blocks from the waters of Lake Michigan on the northside of the river. Located at the corner of State and Superior Streets, today it is surrounded by towering high-rises whose size dwarfs its 210-foot steeple and shining cross of gold. The dimensions and architectural lines of the cathedral

add a genteel civility amid the growing canyons of neighborhood life. Unlike other cathedrals in the United States, this is a fully functioning parish.

An interior remodeling was carried out in 1915 by Henry J. Schlacks to expand the size of the liturgical sanctuary. That paled in

Left: Modern abstract stained glass cathedral windows, fabricated in Milan fashion.

Right: The neo-gothic design of Holy Name is fashioned in yellow Illinois limestone, a stone popular in the years following the Chicago Fire.

comparison to the extensive renovation the cathedral received in 1969 by C.F. Murphy and Associates to incorporate the changes ordered by the Second Vatican Council. At the same time, the building was structurally updated, with a new reinforced concrete foundation replacing the original, the introduction of air conditioning, and a new lower basement. Bronze doors, designed by Albert Friscia, each weighing 1,200 pounds, were sculpted to fit the portal arching of the front entranceway, providing a touch of organic modernity to the neo-gothic façade.

The traditional cruciform interior, 216 feet in length and 102 feet from transept to transept, is covered with the most exquisite element of design within the cathedral—its ceiling. A dizzying display of intricate gilded oak beams and pine lathing, this wooden canopy gives a dramatic sense of warmth and wide-open interior spaciousness. In the wide, uncluttered ecclesiastical minimalism of the sanctuary, the ceiling is enhanced with five dramatically hanging red Roman *galeros*, or broad brimmed cardinal hats, each a reminder of the Archbishops who occupied this sacred space. Emblems of civil authority—the City of Chicago, the State of Illinois, and the United States—are inlaid in wood within the ceiling's vaults. So is the coat-of-arms of John Cardinal Cody, the prelate who renovated the cathedral three decades ago.

The tall, slender stained-glass windows are a stirring, avant-garde mix of form and color without the familiar details of biblical imagery, keeping with the modern artistry introduced in the renovation. The center of focus is the altar, a massive lump of red-black granite, *imperiale de solbrecca,* from Argentina that weighs six tons. It sits upon a rich bronze sculptured pedestal by the

Left: The cathedral interior is rich in gothic arching. At the rear rises the enormous Flentrop organ.

Right: The original cathedral ceiling of gilded oak. Here, three of the five red *galeros* or cardinals' sombreros can be seen hanging from the ceiling.

Below: The Chapel of the Eucharist, designed by Lucca Lucchetti, is part of the massive reconstruction of the cathedral in 1969.

Italian artist Eugenio de Courten. Bronze also is utilized in the five biblical friezes that encircle the sanctuary, depicting references to the Holy Name of Jesus and the traditional Stations of the Cross by Goffredo Verginelli.

Another forceful element of architectural artistry is the vast pipe organ from Flentrop, Holland, that sits in the cathedral's music loft at the west end of the building. Installed in 1989, it is one of America's largest and most powerful pipe organs. The solid French oak organ case is forty-feet high, twenty-eight feet wide. Five large decorative wood towers rise all the way to the top of the interior vaults. To accommodate its mass, the case had to be built around the cathedral's rose window. The instrument looms majestically, though a bit dis-proportionately, in a graceful worship space, as enduring as its unique yellow stone.

Auditorium Building & Theater

Architect: Louis Sullivan and Dankmar Adler

Built: 1886–1890

No building more symbolizes the new Chicago of the last decades of the nineteenth century than the Auditorium Building and Theater at 430 South Michigan Avenue. It was the city's first official skyscraper. The 400-room hotel and office complex with an opera-house style theater with seats for more than 4,000 patrons was the most stunning structure in Chicago when it debuted in 1889. Chicagoans filled with pride when they drank in the eighteen-story building designed by Louis Sullivan and Dankmar Adler. It was created in a fresh modern style that seemed to reflect the direction of the city itself. No structure had ever soared so high before in the city's history.

The construction of the Auditorium Building and Theater marked a historic moment in the architectural life of Chicago. It was Sullivan and Adler's first major partnership commission, and it would prove to be their most enduring. Sullivan was the gifted artist whose passion for design gave shape and grace to the massive stone structure. Adler was the genius engineer whose enlightened understanding made it possible to fashion such a creative building.

The exterior, a straightforward façade of simple but powerful stone, remains reminiscent of the influence of H. H. Richardson, the Boston architect who single-handedly revived the taste for Romanesque architecture in America. It was a style that fit the grandeur of

Right: Iron fire escape latticing down the exterior of the Auditorium Building, in front of Sullivan's refined tripled arched masonry windows.

Far Right: The Congress Parkway façade of the Auditorium Building with theater entrance at ground level.

Sullivan and Adler's revolutionary mixed-use practicality. The Auditorium Building was one of the first buildings in the country to attempt this.

The building's main body rose ten stories, containing the luxury hotel that faced Michigan Avenue, the office wing on Wabash Street, and the theater entrance along Congress Parkway. An eight-story tower rose on top of that, making it the highest point in the city. In addition to an observation deck and commercial tenants, the tower contained Sullivan and Adler's offices.

Three great stone arches form the entrance to the hotel and their design is repeated within the interior lobby that Sullivan filled with an abundance of organic ornamentation. A dramatic oversized staircase ascends through a monumental arch and bends to the second floor. Gold leaf and bright colors made this Chicago's most elegant hotel.

The opera house/theater was acclaimed to have the finest acoustics in the world and was filled with almost magical technologies, such as a hydraulic stage and a prototype air-conditioning system. All of this was the product of Adler, the genius of modern engineering. The building itself stretched his abilities when he had to think of a way in which to balance the settlement of the unusually heavy granite and limestone structure. He devised a complex foundation to equalize the uneven distribution of weight within the complex. It was also necessary for him to fashion a clearer system of interior iron framing that would be able to support the unusually heavy hotel spaces of the dining room and kitchen. The weight was carried on the trusses that rose above the stage and auditorium.

Sullivan made the theater the most beautiful and visually triumphant in the country. Five thousand lights filled the space, together with 150 footlights. Rich wood paneling, ornate decorative

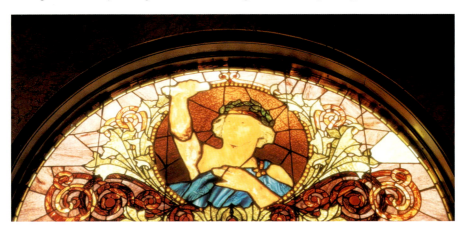

design on moldings around archways and broad plaster friezes all echoed Sullivan's organic, geo-metric, signature ornamental style. His botanical expressions were as dynamic as Adler's invisible engineering feats. Each was a rational expression whose complexity had no precedent.

So sensational was this glittering complex that the Republican Party chose to come there in 1888 for their national presidential convention that ultimately put Benjamin Harrison on the tick-et. One local party official was heard to acclaim the complex, "the biggest thing in the world." In 1893, when Chicago hosted the World's Columbian Exposition, twelve million visitors came to Chicago for the fair held along the south lakefront in Jackson Park. But the most visited site in Chicago, outside the confines of the fair that every visitor made sure to see, was Sullivan and Adler's Auditorium Building. It was an image of modernity and wonder that excited the world.

Sadly, Chicago's tallest building and the world's finest opera house was eclipsed by more modern venues. By 1930, the hotel and theater had hit hard times. The hotel was converted into Chicago's USO center for the duration of World War II and the theater was shuttered. In 1946, the property was purchased by Roosevelt University, who have transformed the hotel and office complex into a bustling urban campus. They have lovingly restored most of Sullivan and Adler's ornaments and fixtures to their original splendor. The Auditorium Theater underwent a total restoration and was reopened in 1967 as bright and brilliant as when it began. It continues as an important venue in Chicago's thriving theater and arts life.

Sullivan and Adler set out with a pragmatic and deliberate purpose to build a palace for the arts and a commercial enterprise to fund it. They wound up with a surprising new architectural expression. "Form follows function" stands not only as their epitaph but their legacy to Chicago.

Left: A stained glass lunette in the tickety lobby, seen against the light.

Right: View across the theater showing the integrated design scheme and the thousands of light bulbs that illuminate it.

Monadnock Building

Architect: Burnham, Root, Holabird, and Roche

Built: 1889–1893

The Monadnock Building at 53 West Jackson Boulevard is a favorite of Chicagoans. It is a rich, textured structure that has deep character and strength. Located just within the footprint of the "L," the elevated train system that once encircled the central business district, this nineteenth-century architectural masterpiece is actually two buildings. The north building, erected between 1889 and 1891, was designed by the Chicago team of Daniel Burnham and John Wellborn Root, two of the city's most strategic architects. The south building, built between 1891 and 1893, was the product of two more critical Chicago architects, William Holabird and Martin Roche. The two wings of the Monadnock Building tell an epic story of American architectural design. So much so, the building is said to be a gateway from one era of American architecture to another. Each reflects a different style not merely in aesthetics but in architectural engineering and form. The difference is visual and tactile, easily seen with the eye, though the two sections are highly complementary to each other.

Burnham and Root's northern section represents the close of one age of design. While sleek and modern in its sophisticated vertical simplicity, these sixteen stories are executed with enor-

mous load bearing walls. The upper weight of the structure, therefore, must be supported

Left: The windows demonstrate the curving sweep of the lower structure and the thickness of the masonry.

Right: The remarkably plain exterior of the structure is enhanced by the geometric arrangement of the windows.

by the strength and mass of the lower section. Beneath the surface, a huge iron and concrete raft holds the massive bulk. Consequently, the walls at the bottom of the building are, by necessity, six-feet thick. The deep recesses created by the girth of the walls hold some of the structure's windows, while elsewhere other windows alternate in pairs or in projected triple bays. The expanding arrangement of the windows themselves becomes a sweeping elegant ornamentation. The beauty of the building's exterior artistry flows from an exquisite tapered movement from bottom to top. In the same way the walls begin to curve above the elevation of the first floor, repeating that curve in reverse, descending from the top. No other external decorative ornamentation is fashioned to compete with this graceful restraint of Root. While this is Chicago's tallest wall-bearing building, it is also its last. The tradition of such voluminous, massive construction was quickly coming to an end in high-rise design. It no longer appeared feasible to go any higher with this kind of masonry design. Sadly, this would be Root's last building that he guided to completion. His death, in 1891, brought his gifted influence to an end.

The southern section, by Holabird and Roche, is built in an entirely different method—it is a skeleton or metal-frame construction. This method reduces the need for the lower portion of the building to bear the weight of the upper mass. The steel frame distributes the weight evenly across the structure. A similar brown brick is employed on exterior walls, as well as a terra-cotta cladding around the steel frame, continuing a similar pattern of projecting window bays as found in the north building. A strong harmony of style results along the Dearborn streetscape. This south addition is equally significant for it marks the introduction of a new and vital tradition in Chicago, the beginning of steel-frame fabrication.

Within the interior of the building are elaborate cast-iron and wrought-iron shapes, elegant stairways, and ornamentation which show both beauty and strength. Period light fixtures continue to hold low-watt bulbs that cast an ocher sheen across the floors. Offices utilize frosted glass doors, and external walls frame windows to maximize interior light. Skylights permit stairways to enjoy added natural light. Offices themselves have elegant bays created by the window recesses and projections. A very graceful late nineteenth-century character further fills the building, having undergone extensive restoration in recent years to return it to its original splendor.

The Monadnock Building takes its name from a mountain in New Hampshire. But in Chicago, it is a name that evokes artistry and harmony on a grand scale. It is emblematic of the Chicago School of architecture, rich in the details of practicality and balanced aesthetics that shaped Chicago's past. The building has long been a home to lawyers, architects, and small merchants who have appreciated its attractive simplicity and historic legacy. This is a building without guile— straightforward and designed for thoughtful and industrious professionals.

The artistry of the Monadnock Building is plain and strong. Its architectural language projects a refined utility and an inner harmony that has never gone out of style. Chicago's most significant nineteenth-century architects created here a unified masterpiece that ripens still with age. Ironically, it sits across Jackson Boulevard on the edge of Mies van der Rohe's acclaimed minimalist Federal Plaza, an arrangement of glass and black steel government buildings that many feel is his masterpiece of urban public space. A remarkable synergy transpires in viewing Monadnock and Mies, one from the other, or in seeing them side- by-side. Each demonstrates the crisp linear verticality of modern utility, though in vastly contrasting materials, and in two different centuries. But the lasting test of the Monadnock Building is its appropriate architectural ability to be complimentary. Monadnock's simple and handsome architectural dexterity comes from its own inner beauty and structural elegance that continues to give shape to Chicago.

Newberry Library

Architect: Henry Ives Cobb

Built: 1892

The Newberry Library sits with an American populist majesty on Chicago's only true European square. At 60 West Walton Street, between Dearborn and Clark Streets, the Newberry is infused with an imposing grandeur that Henry Ives Cobb imparted by his dramatic neo-Romanesque architecture. An independent research library, it opened to the public in 1892.

Cobb was a Chicago wonder story. A graduate of M.I.T. and Harvard University, with a year at the Ecole Des Beaux Art in Paris, he became the toast of the town when he was given the commission to design the most famous house in Chicago in 1881—the Rhine castle home of hotel baron Potter Palmer. It was a gift to his wife, Bertha Honore Palmer, the undisputed queen of Chicago society. Its turrets and massive stone battlements became the center of the city's elite and brought Cobb many commissions, including the University of Chicago's first permanent medieval campus structures. In addition, Cobb was chosen to design the home of the Chicago Historical Society, a massive stone monolith not far from the Newberry. The timeless design of that structure continues to exude historical character, even though it's used as a nightclub today.

Cobb designed the Newberry Library and built it with a vast fortune that had been left for the purpose by one of Chicago's wealthiest real estate tycoons, Walter Loomis Newberry. He used to say that he "bought land by the foot and sold it by the inch." The building was

Right: Commemorative plaque recalling the previous occupant of the land upon which Newberry Library is built, Mahlon Ogden.

Far Right: The south façade of the library displays Henry Ives Cobb's passion for stone architecture of the historical, Neo-Romanesque style.

designed in complete cooperation with the Newberry's first chief librarian, Dr. William Frederick Poole. While Cobb maintained a free hand with exterior detail, Poole set out to build the most perfect and practical of research facilities. Poole had been the longtime head of the Chicago Public Library and brought a wealth of collaborative assistance with him to the task of organizing the Newberry.

Cobb designed a massive palace to learning and research. The façade is said to have been inspired by the twelfth-century French church of Saint Giles-du-Gard. That historical ecclesiastical form is found at the entrance to the library, in its triple-arched Romanesque entry, rich with carved detail within every niche. From there, the design spreads out into a vast rectangular structure seemingly honed from blocks of chiseled pink granite speckled with shards of mica, that permit the building to glisten in the sun.

Cobb's design called for the use of Larimar steel columns, the first building in Chicago to utilize the new material. While the exterior walls are all solid masonry, the interior construction is all steel. Poole's intervention into the format of interior space enshrined his ideas for the correct conditions for a research library. The first story of the structure's exterior walls have rusticated battered walls with large square mullioned windows. The upper stories are not rusticated and have windows enclosed in arches that span the second and third floors, creating a strong sense of verticality and expansive proportion. The façade is rich in historical mullions and traceries within window design and adds to the exotic character of the building's exterior.

Library interiors are vast spaces for public study. The shape, size, and layout of these areas still bear the imprint of Dr. Poole's touch. His vision was for vast reserves of quietude in which to conduct research in the humanities, the Newberry's specialty. Interior space was also planned to house millions of volumes of library holdings. In 1983, the Newberry underwent a vast renovation and building project. Chicago architect Harry Wiese designed a wing specifically to house all the library's collection. Executed in a crisp simplicity of form, the addition was purely functional,

Left: The library windows carry a large portion of Cobb's artistry across the façade, while bringing interior light into reading rooms.

Below: Ornate capitals atop window pillars serve to sustain the weighty massing of heavy masonry construction.

allowing climate control and other technicalities to aid the storage of the library's valuable collection.

In addition, the Wiese renovation restored the building to its original grace, restoring fixtures and details that had undergone unwelcome alteration. In the mid-1990s, a century of ivy was removed so the building's exterior could be cleaned for the first time in its history. At the time it had been reduced by the grime of urban pollution to a foreboding black structure, darkened by time and soot, its bright skin hidden for decades from light. Today, the Newberry Library once again sparkles in the sun and dances with the dream Henry Ives Cobb first envisioned in his design. Despite its serious, overbearing demeanor, the Newberry remains a monument not only to books but also to Cobb's imaginative, historical vision for Chicago on the edge of Washington Square. The Newberry, in addition to being one of America's most prestigious centers of public academic research, is a lasting tribute to Walter Loomis Newberry himself, whose preoccupation with Chicago's growth not only made him rich but also endowed a singular center of learning.

Reliance Building

Architect: Daniel Burnham and John Wellborn Root

Built: 1895

The Reliance Building at 32 North State Street, opened in 1895, is another example of a historic architectural partnership, Daniel Burnham and John Wellborn Root. Their impact on Chicago was decidedly profound and was responsible for a vast array of architectural projects from churches and hospitals to domestic residences and commercial warehouses. But their true legacy to Chicago is found in their pioneer designs for big buildings fashioned in an erudite, modern style. For eighteen years, the pragmatic Burnham and the idealistic Root added to Chicago's growing reputation as a city of sophisticated, refined commercial structures.

By the time the fourteen-story Reliance Building was underway, the young Root was dead. His death was an enduring loss for Burnham who struggled through the project with half a heart. When the astounding structure was opened in 1895, it stood as Root's apotheosis. It was the most memorable expression of their professional partnership, sleeker and more innovative than anyone could have foretold. Fashioned entirely of a metal skeletal frame, it was the doorway to a new era of American architecture. So advanced was its design that no other building in American came close to it. The metal frame of the design liberated the structure from the weighty, heavy stone load-bearing walls of the

Right: Colorful inlaid mosaic tiling was fashionable in 1895 when Burnham and Root built their edgy glass and steel high-rise.

Far Right: The Reliance Building was transformed into the Burnham Hotel in 1999.

past. The building's slender network of exterior metal supports displayed a light, free elegance no one in Chicago had ever seen before. The introduction of large sheets of glass framed between the slender piers and mullions permitted the building to sparkle in the sun. Chicago had its first glass and steel, modern, commercial office building. From this pivotal structure would flow the countless architectural descendants clustered across the urban face of the nation.

The strength that came from the arrangement of a system of rigid steel columns and beams infused the structure with a protective resistance to the wind. The columns were adjoined to steel girders that were deep within the foundation and further provided strength and stability unseen in any building with such thin exterior walls. Chicagoans had their first glimpse of a large-scale glass exterior high-rise surface in the Reliance Building. For many, it seemed to defy gravity when compared to other Chicago high-rise structures.

The building's beauty was as essential as its strength. A decorative, cream-colored terra-cotta is used to clad the very narrow window piers and spandrels across the exterior, embellished with a medieval tracery design. The broad windows have wide fixed panes and narrow, fully-functioning sash windows angled at the sides to catch lakefront breezes. The window treatment creates its own unique Chicago characteristic that provides the structure with its "modern" look and later came to be known the world over as the "Chicago window." They would become a standard feature in Chicago design, widely repeated in the decades ahead. The building is topped with a flat but richly textured terra-cotta cornice.

The building seemed to cease its commercial viability in the late 1960s. A steady decline and

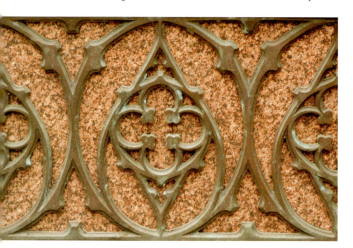

countless interior architectural aberrations seemed to take the spirit from this masterpiece. But its significance to the life of Chicago and its

Left: Detail of the bronze and marble quatrefoil frieze.

Right: Black wrought iron decorative screen.

Far Right: The foyer and elevator bank in the new Burnham Hotel.

influence on the architectural life of America was too important to allow it to wear away. In 1996, the City of Chicago, who had by then acquired ownership of the structure, set out to completely restore the exterior of the building.

In 1998, a consortium of investors acquired the building and totally restored the interior to its original design, discovering treasures hidden for decades. After an exhaustive and reverential refurbishment, the Reliance Building was reborn as the Burnham Hotel in 1999, a part of the Kimpton Group of Boutique Hotels. The 122-room hotel has refreshed State Street and returned the drama of the Reliance Building's unique architectural prominence to the cityscape of Chicago.

The interior of the hotel is thick with restored Burnham artifacts from elevator gratings to inlaid mosaic flooring. A whimsical dining room with premium views of State Street is named the Atwood, commemorating architect Charles Atwood who took Root's place with Burnham in the completion of the building. In the renovation, all the old glass was removed from the windows and replaced with more durable modern glass—all except one. One large window panel remains. Guests and Chicagoans alike are invited to guess which of Burnham's original panes remain.

The significance of the Reliance Building in the history of American architecture is unique. It stands as the direct ancestor of all other glass and steel skyscrapers from coast to coast. A stirring foreshadowing of the future was unveiled when the Reliance Building opened. It brims still with the genius and spirit of Burnham and Root, whose willingness to make no small plans set in motion a new expression in urban commercial design. It would forever change the way cities shape themselves.

Carson Pirie Scott

Architect: Louis Sullivan

Built: 1899

Carson Pirie Scott is a thriving twelve-story department store at One South State Street, Chicago's best-known commercial shopping thoroughfare—"On State Street that great street," Frank Sinatra crooned. Designed by architect Louis Sullivan in 1899, the building is encrusted with the detail and refinement for which Sullivan retains a special Chicago fame. This is a high-use structure at the busiest corner in town—State and Madison Streets. Originally built for the Schlesinger & Meyer Department Store, who commissioned Sullivan for the design, it has been Carson Pirie Scott's flagship store since 1904. In a city of grand architecture, Sullivan created a structure that is both historic and beautiful, being the first large department store to employ fireproof steel-frame construction.

Nothing catches the eye more of Chicagoans and visitors alike than the elaborate two-story cast-iron floral ornamentation that forms the entry canopy to the store. This is a landmark piece of Chicago, like the Art Institute's lions or the clock on Marshall Field's.

Above Right: The geometric pattern of Louis Sullivan's ornamentation is Celtic in its precision.

Right: Polished bronze exterior signage of Carson Pirie Scott.

Far Right: The broad windows of Sullivan's upper-floor exteriors brought unparalleled light into the commercial interior space.

It is an elegant and familiar piece of home located at the very center of the Chicago grid. The city's numbering system, north, south, east, and west, begins at State and Madison Streets, just outside of Carson's front doors. There is a natural geographical primacy to this piece of turf, made more memorable by Sullivan's stately signature iron filigree. This design motif extends south along the State Street windows and east along those on Madison Street. The intricate ornamentation is highly organic, floral, and materially resembles oxidized bronze, a finish that is maintained by layering coats of green paint over red.

Sullivan created a dramatically geometric exterior design, that appears to fan out from the rounded juncture of the exterior walls that ascend above the corner entrance canopy and continues all the way up to the roofline. The building's visual lines are extensively horizontal. This permits the structure to have a refreshingly modern appearance, even before the turn of the century. Sullivan's expansive, broad windows from floors three through twelve are both practical and artistic. They only further enhance the horizontal character of the structure. His broad central panes, flanked on either side by two smaller double panes, permit the store's interior to receive abundant natural light. Outside, spandrels between floors are broad and are brought up flush to the narrow vertical piers. They fashion windows that create an elegant design pattern across the entire structure. Below, ground-floor windows are richly framed in cast-iron and appear wildly modern in their enormity. They permit passing pedestrians the opportunity to see lavish displays of goods without ever entering the store. Sullivan moved window-shopping to a new level. His architecture entices the passer-by.

The building is clad in a rich white terra-cotta, not unlike the Reliance Building down the street. Sullivan makes further decorative use of the terra-cotta with the application of his familiar

Left: Sullivan's fanciful ornamentation was indicative of the Prairie School blend of total simplicity and luxurious excess.

Right: Decorative designs framed Sullivan's sleek architectural lines. Encrusted metalwork was a modern taste that denoted both strength and beauty.

intricate geometric ornamentation on the interior wells of the building's wide window frames. Decoration is subdued but elegant, almost restrained, and further marks the character of the refined commercial establishment within. This is a place, the architecture says, in which you want to shop.

Over the decades the building has expanded to encompass almost the entire block of State Street. The first addition was made by Sullivan himself, when Carson Pirie Scott acquired the store in 1904. Later, Daniel Burnham continued Sullivan's thematic further in 1906. A 1960 expansion by Holabird and Root, further extended the Sullivan façade in a reverential and painstaking manner.

Sullivan has created a timeless Chicago landmark that for more than one hundred years has been an important part of everyday life. Millions of shoppers have passed through his elegant portals, generation after generation. His entryway-rotunda is a spacious and familiar meeting place for people downtown. His design encourages access, movement, and passage through a building that is open and spacious due to the method of steel-frame construction he employed and that runs the length of a city block. He has created visual beauty laden with practical appeal. His modern refinements of style and pragmatic necessity have made this commercial enterprise a showcase of Chicago business. Sullivan was a Chicago visionary whose deceptively simple designs touched both the aesthetic and mundane in everyday living. Sullivan was not a distant intellectual aesthete who built for beauty but lacked the common touches that make public space work. His genius lies in his ability to blend revolutionary architectural design with the necessities of real life. This is what makes him a Chicago favorite and what makes his buildings welcome and familiar to generation after generation of Chicagoans. His work stands the test of time.

Madlener House

Architect: Richard E. Schmidt and Hugh M. G. Garden

Built: 1902

Chicago architects Richard E. Schmidt and Hugh M. G. Garden created one of the city's most elegant and modern domestic residences at 4 West Burton Place, in 1902, for the Madlener family, successful nineteenth-century brewers and Chicago pioneers. It is an urban palace in the heart of the Gold Coast, as the lakefront neighborhood that edges the southern end of Lincoln Park is known. Here, extravagant mansions of quality and taste are a natural part of the landscape. Nearby, the castle of hotel baron Potter Palmer by Henry Ives Cobb once stood. Just one block north is the chimnied Queen Anne residence of the Catholic Archbishop of Chicago designed by Alfred Pashley in 1882. Chicago's most famous architects have always fashioned this neighborhood with dramatic homes and European townhouses. Houses here are noticed and critiqued.

Schmidt fashioned a remarkably restrained three-story structure for the Madleners that has all the elegance of a Renaissance Revival *palazzo* but incorporates the finest details of the famed Chicago School. Both Schmidt and Garden were deeply influenced by Louis Sullivan and Frank Lloyd Wright. At first glance, many think the house to be the work of Louis Sullivan, so flawlessly did Schmidt and Garden affect the daring of his Prairie Style hallmarks. The building has a decidedly geometric, simple cubic-shape. The sight lines are demonstrably horizontal and are a

reminder of the flow Sullivan created at Carson Pirie Scott. From the stone base to the roof, the horizontal lines of the house are

Left: The cube stands as the basic building shape for this Edwardian masterpiece of design.

Right: The central staircase of shimmering Circassian walnut and mahogany has a decidedly Arts and Crafts feel.

accentuated by stone banding. The simple but geometric arrangement of the windows further deepens the horizontal flow.

The exterior of the house incorporates special thin, wheat-colored bricks of the Prairie Style. They are effectively used to induce a fresh, modern appearance. Wright uses a similar style brick around the corner on Astor Street, at the famed Charnley House. Their use by Schmidt brings more than a patina of the period's flourishing Arts and Crafts Movement to the work here. Madlener's grandeur is quiet and respectful, not spilling over into the landscape around it. There is a harmony with natural things. The bold design of the main floor diminishes to a simple geometric arrangement of windows on the second floor and is further restrained and narrowed on the third, housing the home's ballroom.

Garden applied a special architectural artistry in the application of external ornamentation. The entrance way is heavily textured with his incised, geometric limestone frame. These broad bands of decorative ornament are Prairie Style through and through. Though simple against the plainness of the exterior, these designs are spectacular. The doorframe treatment is complimented with an intricate, delicate, bronze grillwork on the front door itself. It is bold and evocative of the linear modernity within the home's interior. The door is not only functionally practical; it becomes a significant feature of exterior ornament.

Within the house, the reserve of the exterior is continued. Restraint is the optimum word. A heavy use of natural materials brings warmth and texture. The first floor is an exotic mix of rare woods. Circassian walnut and close-grained mahogany are generously used in the entrance hall and on the grand staircase. Warm-toned limestone is used for the oversized fireplace in the hall that features entryways to each of the other rooms on this floor. Rooms are large but not

Right: A modern palazzo of Chicago elegance is fashioned in narrow prairie brick and horizontal stone banding.

excessive. They are rectangular and well proportioned. Their shape is their art. The scale of exterior windows seems to mass larger on the interior, adding to the geometry created by the balance between the walls and ceilings. The dining room, located on the front side of the house, looks out to Burton Place, and contains Garden's breathtakingly beautiful cast-plaster, filigree, ornamented ceiling. This interior opulence is complimented by the simple proportions of the room.

Tall, elaborate green and gold art-glass windows rise along the central staircase to the family quarters on the second floor. After the dramatic materials and proportions of the main floor, the practicality of the second floor is surprising. These are rooms for simple necessities and are treated with simplicity. The third floor ballroom and anterooms were an important feature in the Edwardian age. Decidedly elegant in its proportioned simplicity, Schmidt created a grand room for large-scale entertainments. The significant social character of the neighborhood would have made this room indispensable.

In 1963, the Madlener House passed out of family control and many feared it would be doomed to the wrecking ball. Homes like this, in the days before Chicago enacted its tough landmark protection laws, were ripe for extinction and replacement by tasteless period residential high-rises. Fortunately, the Graham Foundation for the Advance Study in the Fine Arts was able to acquire the property. It is now a center for those who treasure the remarkable architectural tradition of Chicago. Schmidt and Garden's masterpiece of domestic Chicago design is safe. The structure received a respectful restoration by the architectural firm of Brenner, Danforth, and Rockwell in the 1980s. The work of Louis Sullivan's disciples endures, a high point of Chicago's Prairie Style.

Wrigley Building

Architect: Graham, Anderson, Probst, and White

Built: 1921–1924

The name Wrigley is attached to three significant elements of Chicago living—chewing gum, Cubs baseball, and the city's most beloved skyscraper. Anyone of these is enough to spark high-pitched debate in a city where each enjoys an unusual competitive variety. But when 1920s elegant modernity weds a world-class, local Chicago business enterprise, and manages to acquire the best building site in town, most real Chicagoans would agree that the Wrigley Building has always had the edge over every other downtown structure.

The Wrigley Building, at 400 North Michigan Avenue, a soaring white terra-cotta masterpiece along the north bank of the Chicago River, was designed and built between 1921 and 1924 by the Chicago architectural firm of Graham, Anderson, Probst, and White, the successor to Daniel Burnham and Company. This is literally, "the house that chewing gum built." Until it was edged out in 1925 by the Tribune Tower, its Michigan Avenue neighbor, this was Chicago's tallest building.

The Wrigley Building is, in fact, two structures. One, a twenty-story south section (thirty-two stories with the tower) and the other, a twenty-one-story north section, set at complimenting angles to each other. The sections appear so unified, many Chicagoans do not realize they are two separate components. The two

Right: A view of the glazed white terra-cotta tower on the twenty-one-story north section of the building taken from the Tribune Tower.

Far Right: The shining white Baroque face of Chicago's most treasured commercial high-rise.

sections are connected at the ground level with a three-story breezeway and at the fourteenth floor with an enclosed skybridge. Rising up from the slightly older southern building is the familiar finger of the famous Wrigley Tower and clock. The tower is an intimate part of the Chicago skyline and has its origins in the elaborate Moorish designs found in the Giralda Tower of Spain's famed fifteenth-century Cathedral of Saville. The two-story clock features four dials, each nineteen feet, seven inches in diameter.

This Spanish Revival motif is continued throughout the exterior of the building, enhanced heavily by the ebullient, Baroque confections that fill the rooflines of each section and the segmented structure of the tower that rises to a height of 425 feet above the street. The glazed terra-cotta tiles are a unique feature of the building's design and appear a dazzling bright white that varies to a bluish cast as they ascend, making them seem even brighter. The façade is rich in ornamental embellishment, executed in the design of the tiles across the spandrels and in the string coursing of the lower floors. The verticality of the building is emphasized by the broad central piers that rise from the entranceway to the tower above. The window arrangements, in patterned pairs and single units, are enhanced by the elaborate and effective use of terra-cotta detail.

At night the east and south façades of the building are illuminated by 116 thousand-watt metal halide lamps, located on the opposite southeast bank of the Chicago River, and sixteen lamps to the west. The Wrigley Building has a powerful Chicago personality and sets the theme for the dramatic streetscape along Michigan Avenue by the sheer beauty of its character. The building enjoys a sophisticated reputation, long the home of advertising agencies, public relations firms, publishers, and consular diplomats. Historically, it was the first commercial high-rise to be

constructed on the north side of the river. It is said that William Wrigley himself chose this site for his business headquarters, feeling the location would give his business empire appropriate

Left: The four two-story clock faces of glazed white terra-cotta tiles stand nineteen feet, seven inches tall.

Above Right: The highly-polished bronze building signage reflects the well-rubbed decorative ornamental bronze of the entrance way.

panache. In addition to the Wrigley Building being a commercial pioneer here, the site is also hallowed ground having been the location of the first domestic settlement in pioneer Chicago, the homestead of Chicago's first citizen, Jean Baptiste Pointe du Sable, at the end of the eighteenth century.

The Wrigley Building sits above the Chicago River on its own manmade palisade. Proximity to the water provides easy access to river taxis below and the tourist boats that traverse the waterway during warm weather. This is a vibrant location, intensified by the drama and imperial splendor of the Wrigley Building's presence. In many ways, it stands as a grand gate to the rest of the city for boat traffic passing beneath the Michigan Avenue Bridge. This building has a special Chicago cache that has set the tone for how the rest of Michigan Avenue developed. It looms in grandeur as a fortress of commercial enterprise whose design well suits its function. The Wrigley Building also suits the aestheticism of Chicagoans who appreciate its elegance and its place in the local landscape. People can understand its architectural language that continues to transmit beauty and strength. It has far more competition today than it did in the 1920s when Michigan Avenue was a boutique reserve for old money. But the Wrigley Building and its architects, Graham, Anderson, Probst, and White, set in place a determined and spectacular sense of architectural proportion that continues to influence the quality and sophistication of local high-rise design. Its historical expression continues the tradition begun long ago in Daniel Burnham's elegant dream for Chicago.

Tribune Tower

Architect: Raymond Hood and John Howells

Built: 1922–1925

The Tribune Tower, at 435 North Michigan Avenue, is a robust and enigmatic component of the Chicago landscape. As the city's most significant daily broadsheet, the *Chicago Tribune* exercises an influence that goes back to pioneer days. When the publisher, Colonel Robert McCormick decided in 1922 to construct a new home for the newspaper, he did so with his usual sense of style and drama. Rather than select an architect cold, McCormick announced that the *Tribune* would sponsor an international competition for its design and he urged all comers to submit their designs for what he termed, "the most beautiful and distinguished office building in the world."

McCormick had already purchased a site for the new structure that met his high demands. The Colonel had three specific needs. The site had to be somewhere at the center of the city. It had to be connected to a switch railroad spur. It had to have easy accessibility to the Chicago River so that newsprint from Canada could be brought in through the lake. He decided on Michigan Avenue, a double- deckered street along the banks of the Chicago River with rail accessibility. All he needed was an architect.

Two hundred and sixty submissions came in from all over the world. Designs came from

Right: A granite cathedral in the sky, the Tribune Tower's neo-gothic architectural lines seem to come from a Medieval era.

Far Right: The flying buttresses stand more than twenty-four stories above street level and enhance the proportions of the stone massing.

Chicago architects as well—especially the proponents of the Chicago School. In the end, McCormick surprised everyone and selected the relatively young and unknown design team of Raymond Hood and John Howells. Their thirty-four-story neo-gothic tower best met the physical operating needs of the newspaper. It was controversial and many were disappointed that McCormick had turned his back on the traditions of Chicago architecture's Prairie modernity. Others felt that Gothic Revival was too historic a style for the flashy 1920s.

Howell and Hood fashioned a tower of elegance and refinement for McCormick. They acknowledged their design was inspired by the famed Tour de Beurre of the French Cathedral of Rouen and the tower of the Malines Cathedral in Belgium. When it was completed in 1925, the Tribune Tower soared thirty-four stories into the Chicago skyline, setting a new record at 463 feet. The tower's frame was made of steel and fireproof concrete. The outer walls were made of variegated shades of gray Indiana limestone. The structure set further Chicago records requiring more than 9,000 tons steel and 12,000 tons of stone, costing $8.5 million.

Hood and Howells used the historic elements of gothic detail to their advantage. In the upper floors of the structure they used enormous flying buttresses as an integral part of the architectural system. They carry the structural piers of the lower portion of the tower up to the ornamental crown on top. They also allow the top to be illuminated at night, adding another dimension to the drama of a thirty-four-story medieval tower across the Chicago skyline.

The Gothic Revival style permitted the architects to embellish the tower with the traditional features of medieval ornamentation, an endless array of gargoyles, grotesques, and animal sculptures. Some have a humorous but ironic symbolism aimed at the very nature of the building's journalists. An owl holding a camera in his claw warns all to be both observant and cautious. Elsewhere, an elephant wearing spectacles holds his nose, and is said to represent scandal, an

Left: The familiar logo of Chicago's most influential broadsheet stands atop what was once the paper's printing plant adjacent to the tower.

Below: A cityscape view from the latticed medieval battlement beneath the Tribune Tower's vaulted crown.

essential element of modern reportage. The building is laced with an endless series of stone monkeys, porcupines, dogs, and ferocious beasts, all the work of master masons depicting the evils and virtues of the world.

The interior of the tower is a refined modern office complex, diminutive and quaint by twenty-first century standards, but richly appointed by the hand of Colonel McCormick. The *Chicago Tribune* remains one of the world's great newspapers. All around its lobby, massive slabs of stone carry the historic words of statesmen and authors, patriots and heroes. Lincoln's Gettysburg

address is carved into a wall of granite near the base of the flying buttresses on the twenty-fourth floor deck. Also prominently displayed in stone are the Colonel's own words spoken at a World War I battlefield reunion at Cantigny, in France.

The Tribune Tower is an important architectural landmark. Together with its Wrigley Building neighbor, it forms a dramatic architectural gateway to the significantly expanded Michigan Avenue commercial district. Though the Tribune Tower's design recalls a period many centuries removed from contemporary living, its graceful character long ago became thoroughly Chicago.

35 East Wacker Drive

Architect: John Giaver and Frederick Dinkelberg

Built: 1926

The ivory-colored wedding cake-like tiers of the 35 East Wacker Drive Building made a powerful statement in the skyline of Chicago from the day it first opened in 1926. It represented an unprecedented expansion in the commercial high-rise properties in the city and served as an exciting indicator of the financial health of Chicago business. Its extravagant neo-Baroque design was the work of two Chicago architects, John Giaver and Frederick Dinkelberg, who had their start in the firm of Daniel Burnham and Company. They set out to make nothing less than a spectacular statement in the already established, but fresh, urban multi-storied terrain.

Originally known as the Jewelers Building, Giaver and Dinkelberg's creation was an architectural wonder perched high above the

Left: The angel-topped bronze clock at the corner of Wacker Drive and Wabash Street.

Right: This terra-cotta office tower once had an indoor parking system that permitted tenants to drive to their office via a unique automobile elevator.

south bank of the Chicago River. It was a twenty-four-story super structure, topped by a seventeen-story tower, each heavy with ornamentation, but light with a supremely soaring vertical line. At first glance, the building expresses its strength with an imposing character detailed in the four classically-styled temples standing at the four corners of the main lower section of the structure. Domed and columned, these cupolas reflect in miniature the much grander scaled temple at the very top of the tower. Chicagoans were intrigued by the forty-foot glass dome at the tower's summit, complete with an observation deck and a fancy restaurant called the Stratosphere. At forty-stories, the Jewelers Building was the tallest building in America outside of New York.

The steel-framed structure is clad in a rich, ivory-colored terra-cotta. Like the nearby Wrigley Building, the decorative embellishments here have a confectionary quality to them that renders an extravagant Rococo feeling. What saves this design is the strength and balance of the building's proportions. Alternating narrow and wide piers give definition to the vertical rise. This enhances the windows, arranged in a double pairing across the face of the structure, with single windows framing the outer edges at each level from the sixth to the eighteenth floor. There, windows are rounded to give the vertical rise a sense of uniformed completion. The pattern is repeated in the tower. Lush, decorative classical cornices create an ornamental line at the top of the main building and at the top of the tower beneath the dome. At street level, granite piers along the façade rise to include four floors of broad, tripartite casement windows, as well as three two-story framed arched windows above the entryway.

Nothing caught the imagination of tenants and interested Chicagoans more than the imaginative indoor parking plan, the first building in Chicago to include such parking in its design. It was said that while the exterior of the building was historical, the interior was its real contribution to modern urban innovation. Because the building had been designed to attract local jewelers and gem merchants, tenants could drive their cars into a garage entrance off Lower Wacker Drive and into a special automobile elevator in the core of the building that carried them in their car directly up to a space outside their office on their floor. It was advertised as a special security precaution, but never really succeeded in attracting jewelers. After some fourteen years, the idea was abandoned and the elevator space was converted into office space.

It was not long before the idea of having all the city's jewelers in one high-rise was acknowledged as a failure. When the Pure Oil Company signed a long-term lease the same year the building opened, for five full floors of office space, the building's name changed to the Pure Oil Building. Like most new Chicago high-rises constructed in the late 1920s, it was not long before the downturn in the national economy affected the viability of such majestic office complexes like Giaver and Dinkelberg's 35 East Wacker. But it has miraculously weathered the forces of history, thriving today with renewed Chicago architectural significance. Among the most prestigious present tenants is the architectural firm of Murphy and Jahn. The noted Helmut Jahn himself has discovered the remarkable glory of the observation dome. Today it is his architectural studio. It is there, in the shadow of the old Stratosphere restaurant, that clients are presented with their design plans by this world-famous architect.

35 East Wacker Drive remains a startlingly beautiful piece of Chicago architectural history. It presides in state today, during another boom in Chicago architectural development, mindful of the important role it played in shaping the Chicago skyline in the Jazz Age and the wide attention it drew to the city's riverfront.

Chicago Board of Trade

Architect: John Holabird and John Wellborn Root, Jr.

Built: 1930

The Chicago Board of Trade is a furtive expression of Chicago's prairie character. The buying and selling of grains and crops have been a stock component of the city's heartland economy since pioneer times. While the days when grains and corn were stacked high along the river are long gone, the tumult of dealing has not disappeared, only its address has changed. Today, the adventure and drama of commodity trading and futures brokering takes place in the refined Art Deco splendor of the Chicago Board of Trade at 141 West Jackson Boulevard. This splendid forty-five-story tower designed by John Holabird and John Wellborn Root, Jr., each an heir to a wide legacy of Chicago architectural significance, was completed in 1930.

The gray limestone throne-like tower that is home to the Chicago Board of Trade looms high above the canyons of LaSalle Street, Chicago's financial district, soaring vertically from its base up to the very symbol of the grain exchange, the thirty-two-foot aluminum statue of Ceres, the ancient Roman goddess of grain by sculptor John Storr. The façade consists of two symmetrical

thirteen-story projections that create deep setbacks on both the east and west front section of the building. The Chicago Board of Trade has

Left: The thiry-two-foot statue of Ceres continues to preside with a special grandeur over LaSalle Street.

Right: The building frames the financial district with a high Art Deco style.

arguably the city's most exqui-site Art Deco architecture inside and out. Alternating pro-portions of the structure's tall continuous piers, from wide to narrow, give the building enor-mous verticality and lift. The horizontal lines are constrained, minimized by the use of discontinuous recessed spandrels.

Holabird and Root set the Chicago Board of Trade on a nine-story base that originally includ-ed a six-story trading room, later split in two in 1975 to form the Chicago Board of Options Exchange. Two further additions placed behind the present structure contain massively more expansive trading rooms than could have been envisioned in the 1920s.

Exterior ornamentation is reserved and limited, permitting the slender angularity of the design itself to decorate the façade. Above the entranceway, high over the original trading floor, a large clock sits facing north, flanked on either side by two carved limestone personifications of wheat and corn, rich with Art Deco symmetry. They are the work of Illinois artist Alvin Meyer.

As simple as the exterior ornamentation appears, the interior design is intensified, though equally balanced, and extravagant in the luxury of materials used. The three-story lobby is a mas-terpiece of Art Deco with its passion for sleek, polished surfaces and contrasting marble finishes. Soft light sheens and shimmers off fixtures of translucent glass and nickel, two indispensable ingredients of the period's artistry. Ornamentation is rectilinear, crisp, geometric, and modern. It creates emblematic images of the age of fast ocean liners and silver bullet trains. There is an added flavor of Egyptian influence within the building's interior, expressed in a zigzag decorative pattern. Stainless-steel rails and white bronze cornices blend with black marble and scalloped cream marble to deepen the vertical sight lines that appear angular, curvaceous, and well bal-anced. This is aristocratic modernism at its utilitarian best, utilized in a high volume public space.

The majestic architecture of the Chicago Board of Trade is never more impressive than at night, when it shimmers in an illuminated golden light that emphasizes its graceful modern form.

A bold magnificence of place unfolds at the bottom of the LaSalle Street canyon. It is a unique posture dramatically enhanced by the streetscape's termination at the foot of the Board of Trade's Jackson Boulevard entrance. Holabird and Root's triumph shapes the personality of the neighborhood. Neither the neoclassical Acropolis of the Federal Reserve Bank or the columned glory of the former Continental Bank, each a neighbor along LaSalle Street, reach the heights of architectural supremacy that the Chicago Board of Trade enjoys. It is a flawless expression of both the era, its design, and the significant commercial enterprise that occurs within it every day. In addition to the countless auxiliary services and businesses related to the industry of the Board of Trade, the building also houses tenants in a variety of other financial enterprises.

The Chicago Board of Trade expresses its power and strength through its architectural posture. It is a totem to the viability of Chicago's markets expressed in stone.

Above Left: The true Art Deco grandeur of the interior is displayed in the three-story wonder of the foyer and has no rival.

Left: The geometric flourishes and shimmering surfaces of interior artistry are high expressions of Art Deco design.

Merchandise Mart

Architect: Graham, Anderson, Probst, and White

Built: 1930–1931

The Merchandise Mart is a Chicago landmark with a provenance as sturdy and titanic as its towering appearance. The fact that it spans two full city blocks is just the first indication that this is a structure of dramatic purpose and intensity. It is the remarkably sleek geometry of Graham, Anderson, Probst, and White's design that makes this 1930 jewel of Chicago commerce an anchor in the architectural integrity of riverfront development and success.

Built by Chicago business blueblood Marshall Field of department store and newspaper publishing fame, the 4,100,000 square-foot structure was the largest building in the world when it was completed in 1931 along the Chicago River at Wolf Point, once the center of fur trading in the city's pioneer days. Today, only the Pentagon exceeds its size, though the Merchandise Mart is still the largest commercial building and the largest wholesale marketing center on the planet. Each floor measures more than 250,000 square feet of commercial space. The building's simple geometric form belies the stirring excess of its proportions and interior structural design. Fashioned with a sleek angularity and ennobled by rich modern Art Deco textures, the twenty-five-story building stands 340-feet tall.

Chicagoans are happy with this giant architectural masterpiece, though it was considered

Right: The building's remarkable geometry is displayed in the tower turrets that sit atop each of the building's four corners.

Far Right: The waters of the Chicago River pass the south façade of the Mart.

quite a stretch in the 1920s, especially for Graham, Anderson, Probst, and White, whose cautious architectural conservatism had never before produced anything quite so radically modern. It is a building of unusual architectural anonyms—massive but sleek, squat but trim. Proportionality is the hallmark of its design, achieved by an expansive vertical sweep that is pure perfection. At ground level, a broad plaza recesses the structure in from the riverbank. A three-story entranceway of deliberate and vast excess visually alters the perspective of the façade. Above it rises the structure's central tower that both defines the vertical sweep and divides the east and west sections into two further cubes. Four scaled, low, geometric towers rise slightly from the four corners of the building, further defining the proportions of the cube. Conspicuous piers and dark recessed spandrels accentuate the streamline verticality of the overall flow. The geometric indenting of upper floors and the rounding of window wells provide an additional sense of strength and completion to the linear rise. The sheer width and mass of the building's face deepens the subtle optical intensity of Graham, Anderson, Probst, and White's classical balance and expression.

The rich, evocative details of Art Deco design are intensified within the Merchandise Mart's interior. As befits the largest commercial building in the world, the lobby is a mass of open space and vertical drama. Bright black and cream marble surfaces, streamline escalators to mezzanines and high ceilings are emblematic of the elegance that is the signature of Art Deco style. Colorful inlaid marble floors are emblazoned with the MM monogram, a logo repeated throughout the interior. Upper floors are glass windowed showrooms closed to the general public. The commerce here is strictly wholesale. The 8.5 miles of interior corridors are labyrinthine, an endless series of long halls and passageways that run past miles and miles of displays and showcased wholesale merchandise. The trade here is for the smart set, both in style and economics. More than two

Left: The scale of the grand entranceway gives the building a human perspective and fresh modernity that is critical to the largest commercial structure in the world.

Right: Bronze busts line the parapet of the Merchandise Mart honoring the greats of local commerce in the Chicago Retail Hall of Fame.

thousand lines of furniture, fabrics, floor covering, bathroom fixtures, antiques, and interior fashion accessories are located within the complex. The Merchandise Mart is also the world's oldest design center, another legacy of Marshall Field.

Joseph P. Kennedy, the scion of the Boston political family, purchased the Merchandise Mart from Marshall Field in 1945, providing Chicago with a unique Kennedy connection. Though the family no longer owns the building, a Kennedy grandson still oversees the facility. A renovation between 1986 and 1991 refreshed the building and expanded its retail space with the introduction of a two-story street-level shopping mall. In addition to the thousands who work at the building, retail shoppers are now to be found in the thousands of new residents who populate the Merchandise Mart's "River North" neighborhood.

The Merchandise Mart is an important Chicago building. It is not like other office high-rises, either in its structural proportions, architectural significance, or in its purposeful commercial character. The building is special to Chicagoans. The Mart's robust size and burly attitude probably strikes a familiar chord with the Chicago residents. Perhaps its fortress-like personality exudes a strength and stability that is comforting and protective. A clue is to be found in its utilitarian purpose, so centered on enterprise, commerce, and honest effort. Perhaps it is beloved because it is so beautiful and uncomplicated in its streamlined style. The Merchandise Mart flowed from the imagination of architect Ernest Graham, who as a very young man worked with Daniel Burnham on the World's Columbian Exposition of 1893. His firm became the architectural heir of Burnham's legacy. Perhaps Chicagoans love his Merchandise Mart because, like Burnham, it is fused with such practical grace.

LaSalle National Bank

Architect: Graham, Anderson, Probst, and White

Built: 1934

Even just a quick walk through the lobby of the LaSalle National Building, at 135 South LaSalle Street, is enough to engulf the visitor in the sights and textures of the most splendid Art Deco detail in Chicago. For many, this treat would be a surprise. This remarkable building, originally built by Marshall Field in 1934 as the headquarters for the Field family's vast financial enterprises, is a less well-known Chicago architectural treasure. This does not have the public reputation, recognition, or notoriety of the Sears Tower, the Auditorium, or the Board of Trade. Designed by Graham, Anderson, Probst, and White, this is not a building that everyday Chicagoans know by sight, much less by the elaborate modernity of its public space. Its thoroughly modern limestone exterior has no external ornamentation. There is little to catch the eye, except the exquisite vertical lines of its majestically modern sweep. Few Chicagoans might also know that this soaring structure of pure Art Deco simplicity sits on sacred architectural ground—the site of the city's very first skyscraper, William LeBarron Jenny's steel-framed Home Insurance Building of 1885.

Known originally as the Field Building when it was completed, Field had offered the architects a similar challenge to the one he gave for the design of his Merchandise Mart—the largest office

building in the city. At forty-five-stories and one city block in width, stretching from Clark Street to LaSalle Street, he was well pleased. With more than 1,000,000 square feet of rentable floor

Left: White bronze Art Deco clock featured in the first floor lobby between Clark and LaSalle Streets.

Right: The exterior of the LaSalle National Bank is devoid of any external ornamentation. Its grandeur is expressed in the crisp geometric lines of its Art Deco simplicity.

space, it was, indeed, Chicago's largest commercial high-rise. Measuring 435 feet in height, it was also Chicago's tallest structure and boasted the largest and most elegant elevator bank in the city. The exterior, however, was almost Puritan in its incredible ornamental restraint. So edgy was its design that it was without embellishment, permitting its vertical character to speak its announcement of the arrival of a fresh new neighbor to the Chicago skyline. Its simplicity, like other past expressions of Chicago architectural design, was bold and aristocratically brash.

The building's structural form actually resembles a bundle of granite blocks, a forty-five-story central tower sitting in the middle of four smaller towers of twenty stories each. The construction took place in stages with the center tower completed last. The linear proportions of the towers are intensified by the vertical bands and narrow windows that define the Art Deco character of the exterior structure. Chicago had never seen anything so visually pure. It would have to wait twenty-five more years for Mies van der Rohe.

Before the building could be completed, the Great Depression engulfed the nation. But the project went full steam ahead. The construction of the Field Building was one of the few bright spots in the trades, employing union workers at a time when there was little work. As the structure reached completion, it was announced that the building's management would accept only new firms or new branches as tenants, so as not to ruin the occupancy of other Chicago buildings during the crisis.

No Chicago high-rise was given a grander interior that the Field Building, an effusive

Far Left: The shimmering lobby of the LaSalle National Bank is a high mark of Art Deco design. Its marble surfaces and white bronze bridges and lighting fixtures are emblematic of Jazz Age style.

Below Left: The linear white marble cladding of the lobby gives vertical lift to the geometry of interior shapes.

Right: A white bronze decorative eagle fashioned in the Art Deco style adorns the U.S Postal box within the lobby.

display of Art Deco design. The block-long two-story lobby is encrusted with fluted pilasters of creamy white marble and recessed panels of beige Italian marble. Cream colored terrazzo is used on the floor and nickel silver accents abound. Above the lobby, shining nickel bridges link the north and south balconies of the mezzanine. Slender embellishments and opulent linear forms sparkle. The city's largest Art Deco lobby recalls the grandeur of a past age, imperial in its reserve, like the first-class dining room aboard the great French liner *Normandie*. The cosmetic perfection here runs deep. The most stunning ornamental detail is the elevator indicator panel and mail drop that recreates the building itself in miniature. Etched glass and nickel silver are used throughout for signage.

When the building opened, it boasted the latest technological advances from an air-conditioned restaurant to a central vacuum cleaning system within the offices. The building's five private dining rooms, three bars, and two oyster bars were a mark of the refined character of the environment.

With the construction of this remarkable building, Chicago saw its last new commercial high-rise for twenty-five years. It would be more than a decade after World War II before the skyline of the Loop would have a new addition. Today, the building is known as the LaSalle National Bank and enjoys a fresh appreciation of its architectural significance. The building remains a timeless expression of elegance, architectural restraint, and purity of form.

860/880 North Lake Shore Drive

Architect: Ludwig Mies van der Rohe

Built: 1949

These are the buildings that began both Chicago's great post-war architectural revolution and firmly established Ludwig Mies van der Rohe as the father of a second Chicago School of architectural design. These two deceptively simple twenty-six-story glass and steel apartment buildings along the shore of Lake Michigan might, at first glance, resemble a long line of other black steel and glass towers in any number of America cities. But the resemblance is only skin deep. This is where it all erupted in 1949, when the German-born architect heading Chicago's Illinois Institute of Technology School of Architecture translated his vision of the International School style into the sleek, unembellished, rectangular boxes that ultimately became his signature design. Chicago would never be the same. The impact was profound.

Mies introduced the vocabulary of new architectural language to the city—glass curtain, structural I-beams, blackened steel—"Less is more." With the construction of 860/880 North Lake Shore Drive, the arrival of the modern style could not be denied. It fused this new expression in high-rise architecture into the soul of the city. For generations, Lake Shore Drive has been

Chicago's most exclusive and public streetscape. The introduction of this modernist style was jarring to many, especially

Left: Glass lobby interior includes furniture designed by Mies van der Rohe.

Right: The twin glass and steel residential towers unleashed modern architecture in post-war America in 1949.

those content with the historic character of past styles that were so prevalent around this neighborhood's exclusive residential buildings. But for people with wider tastes, the style was as
luscious as their first espresso.

The new buildings were all about simplicity of style, letting the materials create a living space
that was flexible and proportioned—the classical technique of successfully employing balance and
optical perception. The buildings were also about the freedom that the post-war world was looking for in every element of living. The Miesian approach appeared to be a further expression of
that philosophical aesthetic. In the design of the 860/880 North Lake Shore Drive Apartments,
the architect exposed the structural frame of the building, running I-beams up the outside of the
building for the full vertical length. These unembellished surfaces framed the glass panels that
served as the exterior walls of the structure. Within the interior, he designed a skeleton frame
containing a utility shaft down the central core. The result was unobstructed interior space for
modern living with total flexibility. Interior apartment walls are moveable to contour themselves to
the needs of the tenant. The exterior black skin of the steel beams provided a further detail of
modern simplicity known as minimalism. It became a word with its own Chicago meaning—subtle-
ty and flexibility. It marked a new age of Chicago design.

Mies set the buildings perpendicularly, at right angles to one another, forty-six feet apart,
providing each with maximum exposure to Chicago's greatest natural wonder, the ever-changing
panorama of Lake Michigan. The lakefront was the perfect site for such engaging minimalism.
Expansive views were abundant in every direction from the glass curtain that encircled
each apartment.

Within the building's public interior space, the tall glass-encased lobby, more Miesian touches appear. They too emphasize the minimalist persona. Mies' chrome and leather Barcelona chairs, named for their inclusion in the 1929 International Exposition in that Spanish city, are arranged with matching ottomans and glass tables. The furniture fits the simplicity of Mies' "Glass Houses," as the lakefront dwellings were soon known.

Chicagoans, today, take the minimalism of Mies van der Rohe as a constituent part of every-day life. His designs for commercial high-rise structures intertwine the city's streets and constitute some of its most important architecture. His expansive Federal Plaza, IBM Building, and two further Lake Shore Drive apartment buildings are just a portion of his architectural lega-cy to the city. His influence upon succeeding generations of Chicago architects can be seen across the urban skyline, not only in Chicago, but also across America. The glass and steel sky-scraper has become synonymous with modern American architecture. But it is hard to imagine what it must have been like in 1949 to glimpse these buildings for the first time.

It is no accident that Miesian minimalism found a comfortable fit in Chicago. The city's long enduring delight in architecture of challenge and substance predisposed it for its passionate affection for modern design. The utility of Miesian architecture had special appeal to erudite sophisticates and everyday people alike. They are comfortable places in which to live and work. Miesian modernism shapes the contours of local courtrooms, post offices, law firms, and schools. His touch is profound and long lasting. His controversial style fit into a deep local history of edgy architectural designs from Daniel Burnham and Frank Lloyd Wright to Helmut Jahn.

Left: The black painted steel and glass of Mies van der Rohe became his American signature.

Right: Glass and steel simplicity was a radical architectural expression when these towers were first built. Today they are a familiar part of the landscape.

Inland Steel Building

Architect: Skidmore, Owings, and Merrill

Built: 1958

The shimmering stainless steel and green glass Inland Steel Building at 30 West Monroe Street is perhaps Chicago's most significant post-war commercial high-rise office building. It began a renaissance in commercial office construction being the first such skyscraper to be built in the city since the Great Depression. This nineteen-story office tower designed by Skidmore, Owings, and Merrill is small by Chicago standards at 332-feet. Both the LaSalle National Bank Building and the Chicago Board of Trade dwarf this addition to the local skyline. But what remains remarkable about this particular building is its graceful proportions and its restrained detail, so elegantly flashed in the demonstrably bold modernist style. It was a model for the future of Chicago architecture.

Inland Steel's decision to build their national headquarters in Chicago was an important commercial investment in the city. Their further decision to approve a structure in the modernist style was an equally significant investment. The style, ironically, offered the steel company a unique opportunity to showcase their own product in the fabrication of their corporate office tower. Steel, rather than traditional concrete, was also utilized in the construction of the structure's foundation, with piling

· **Right:** The overhang of the Inland Steel Building projects over the pedestrian right-of-way.

Far Right: The silver steel frame and aqua tint glass marked the first commercial high-rise building in Chicago since the 1930s.

Left: Gleaming stainless steel columns were a structural detail that continue to brighten the Chicago skyline.

Below Right: Modern architecture achieved an aesthetic triumph that was both utilitarian, innovative, and also dramatically beautiful.

extending some eighty-five feet to the bedrock. It was the first such building in Chicago to make use of this method. On Skidmore, Owings, and Merrill's part, Bruce Graham and Walter Netsch, two important Chicago architects, served as principal designers of the project that marked their firm's first significant downtown high-rise. It marks the start of their enormous influence on the city's architecture that includes the Daley Center, the John Hancock Center, and the Sears Tower.

The building made use of highly imaginative structural details. Seven gleaming exterior columns running the vertical length of the building's nineteen floors were responsible for carrying the entire weight of the structure. Within the frame structure of the interior the floors were supported by sixty-foot girders that ran the horizontal length of the building. Windows in a deep shade of aquamarine green were extended from the ceiling to three inches from the floor. Because all the structural support came from the exterior wall of the structure, the interiors of the office floors incorporated a plan layout of enormous flexibility. Interior space was unencumbered by mechanicals and service apparatus. A separate tower adjoining the office tower contained its elevators, stairways, and service facilities.

The Inland Steel Building was a design triumph whose snazzy pizazz tantalized Chicago tastes. The public delighted in the exterior elegance, in its mix of stainless steel and cool green glass. They appreciated both the innovation and the functionalism of the design. This building looked like a great place to work. Since it had been twenty-five years since the last office high-rise rose in Chicago, an entire generation had never even seen a new building downtown. In the mid-1950s, the public thrived on the long list of modern firsts that were a part of the structure's design. This was Chicago's first commercial high-rise to use exterior steel support columns; the first to use glass and steel as their chief building materials; the first to have indoor, below-ground parking, and the first to be fully air-conditioned.

A significant dimension to the shaping of public space at the Inland Steel Building concerns the treatment of the streetscape. This was an essential component of their design frame. Dearborn and Madison Streets are traditionally a busy intersection with a heavy traffic flow. Great attention was given to the pedestrian movement on the sidewalks surrounding the building. When your walls are transparent, the activity outside becomes a important consideration. The architects took this new fact of modernist life into consideration and created a sensitive and open streetscape that the building's beauty enhanced, and expanded sidewalk space made inviting. The street level two-story entrance is recessed along the ground creating a sidewalk overhang as the building extends at the third floor becoming a canopy above part of the Monroe Street walkway.

The Inland Steel Building is as bright and fresh as the day it opened forty-three years ago. Its glass curtain and shining stainless steel continue to dazzle. Since the construction of the expansive Bank One Plaza (originally the First National Bank of Chicago) on the opposite side of Dearborn Street in 1969, the view from the western windows of the Inland Steel Building has greatly improved. Below sits Mark Chagall's mosaic wall, *The Four Seasons*.

The architectural landscape of commercial Chicago architecture was forever altered by the modernist design of this singular beauty. Its sophisticated and innovative design was a foretaste in 1958 of wondrous things to come.

Marina City

Architect: Bertrand Goldberg

Built: 1964

When Marina City, Chicago's most edgy experiment in urban residential living, was completed in 1964 by Chicago architect Bertrand Goldberg, at 300 North State Street, it stirred up an enormous fury. Nothing like it had ever been seen in Chicago. It was not just a building, or two; it was a new concept in what cities could be. It frightened people architecturally, and it frightened them philosophically. Boldly, its space-age design seemed to say that cities were a-changing. This was Goldberg's "city within a city." Compact. Contained. Lunar. He offered another perspective in his architecture showing what the urban landscape could possibly become. Woven into his twin sixty-story concrete towers were all the necessities of life—a river marina, a grocery store, a spiral garage, residential living space, office space, restaurants, a theater, an art gallery, a bowling alley, a skating rink, and a swimming pool—all the ingredients of early 1960s living. Goldberg underscored the debate when he said, "I am trying to modify society through architecture."

Marina City was the world's largest concrete structure when it was built, and continues to be the largest in the United States. Concrete was an important

Left: The scalloped shape of Marina City's design was unlike anything in memory.

Right: The twin towers are said to resemble two corncobs, a not unrealistic metaphor for Chicago's heartland roots.

Left: The central core of the twin sixty-story towers protrudes above its roofline and pie wedge balconies.

Right: These circular discs are the essential building blocks for the towers as demonstrated here in the lower eighteen floors of residential parking.

material for Goldberg; it was pliable and easy to maneuver. It was a material for the proletariat, not for the elite—no wonder people were scared. Goldberg bent concrete into imaginative forms but nothing ever so intriguing as Chicago's 580-foot double "corn-cobs," on the river, as they have been characterized. Though Goldberg is often referred to as a "modernist" and though he studied at the Bauhaus in Germany when Mies was there, his work is not reflective of Mies at all. In fact, Goldberg's work presents an alternative to the International Style. His work resembles more the Spanish architect Antonio Gaudi, famous for his work at the Cathedral of Barcelona. Marina City richly displays that passion for curvaceous concrete.

The structure of Marina City is shaped, initially, by its internal core, clearly seen protruding above the roofline of each structure. These cylinders run down through the center of each building supporting the main weight of the tower with circular discs, or slabs, resting on interior columns. From this, the floors fan out; and from this the apartments acquire their curious pie-shape interiors. This structural method extends out to the semi-circular, cantilevered balconies and gives each tower their scalloped crenellation. This slab method construction, as it is known, is more readily visible in the eighteen floors of parking within each building.

When Goldberg initially proposed his design for Marina City's mixed-use, a concept very much in vogue worldwide now, Chicago had a prohibitive zoning ordinance against the very concept of combining residential, retail, and office space within the same building. It was the first of many hurdles his architecture had to overcome. Cities were not popular places to live in the early 1960s. It was the age of suburban flight. Goldberg's Marina City was a challenge to rethink the use of urban space. It was his attempt to re-establish a sense of cohesive urban community many years before the present boom of reverse flight. The arrangement of domestic living space within the towers encouraged a sense of high-rise neighborhood with communal laundry, play space, and storage facilities built around the building's core.

Marina City is not Chicago's most famous building, or its most beautiful, though it might be its most imaginative. But it is a synthesis structure, the product of a philosophical understanding of Chicago's urban environment. Marina City is after all a cocoon, a nest in which to be both secure in the urban landscape and at the same time to be easily connected to nature. Marina City's river location is critical to its initial concept of connection to the nature around it. From its marina, the locks to the mouth of Lake Michigan are just minutes away to the east. Today, four decades after its construction, Marina City has received a big facelift inside and out. Smith and Wollensky's steak house is now the building's high-end restaurant and the House of Blues operates both a club and a hotel within the building's original annex complex.

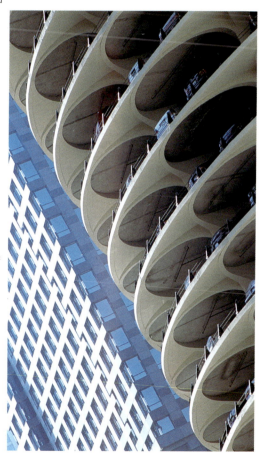

Much of Goldberg's dream for a new rational urbanity to the city's downtown living has come to pass. Few amenities for everyday living existed around the footprint of Marina City when it first challenged local architectural sensibilities. But today, almost forty years later, Marina City is dwarfed by the explosion of new urban domestic residences that have transformed the commercial heart of Chicago into a very heavily mixed-use environment. The urban pavements have been softened by the children of urban flight who find downtown Chicago living dynamic and resourceful. Marina City was, in the end, decades ahead of its time—futuristic some might even say.

Sears Tower

Architect: Skidmore, Owings, and Merrill

Built: 1974

Chicago's most recognizable structure, without doubt, is the Sears Tower. For more than twenty years, its 110-stories made it the tallest building in the world, at least until 1997, when the Petronas Tower in Malaysia nosed it out with the addition of its 111-foot spires. Much controversy marked this international decision. It had little meaning in Chicago. Though the Sears Tower remains the tallest building in North America and has no competition as the world's highest occupied floor or largest skyscraper, at four and a half million square feet, these are minor accomplishments in the Chicago scheme of things. While these architectural superlatives have importance, the meaning of the Sears Tower's enormity must be seen within the evolving context of quality architecture in Chicago.

The Sears Tower, 233 South Wacker Drive, is the architectural child of Skidmore, Owings, and Merrill, the Chicago architectural firm whose influence in modern Chicago is without equal. Like the towering John Hancock Center, built just seven years earlier, the Sears Tower had its beginnings in the imagination of two of Skidmore's most fertile men of vision, architect Bruce Graham and designer-engineer Fazlur Kahn. Graham created the designs and Kahn made

Right: Three of the upper "bundled tiers," or towers, that give the Sears Tower its distinctive verticality.

Far Right: Its sleek black steel and bronze glass dominates the skyline from every direction.

them stand in the wind. Nothing challenged their abilities more than the complex detail required for the greatest high-rise in the world.

The best way to understand the Sears Tower's design is to imagine a pack of cigarettes in which nine individual cigarettes are lifted up above the rest. Two emerge to a mid-level, two are pulled out slightly higher, three are pulled out even further, and the final two are pulled out higher than all the rest. This was Fazlur Kahn's challenge—to build nine towers, all connected, all bundled together for strength. Imagine these cigarettes each to be seventy-five-feet square. Out of this massive "bundled-tube," the Sears Tower was born.

In real life, all nine bundled-tubes rise together in the Sears Tower construction up to the forty-ninth floor. Two stop here. The remaining seven tubes continue to the sixty-fifth floor. Two more discontinue rising here. The remaining five now ascend to the ninety floor, where three stop. The final two tubes now rise to the 110th floor.

Twenty-eight acres of black aluminum are used to fashion the exterior frame of the tower. This is a familiar Chicago high-rise material; the local skyline is thick with elegant examples of structures that its ebony cladding have made well known. The windows are fashioned of a special bronze-tinted glass. The steel frame and glass curtain-style design is a reminder of the many examples of modernist high-rise artistry across the city, none more poetic than the first, another Bruce Graham building, Inland Steel. The tower has nine self-contained vertical sections with soaring piers, graceful setbacks, and sleek, slender, modern lines. For all its mass, the structure

has the crisp sense of skyscrapers of the 1920s. The tower is 1,454 feet tall, 380 feet taller than any of its Chicago competitors.

The Sears Tower was originally built as the headquarters of Sears Roebuck and Company. The building's staggered towers reflect Sears' initial request for occupancy of

Left: For almost three decades, Sears Tower has been the city's best architectural attraction.

Right: The entrance to the Sears Tower, a self-contained city that houses ten of thousands of working people, still boasts of the world's highest elevator ride.

large lower floors to meet their corporate necessities, while allowing allocation of smaller space, as needed, for rental tenants. The building covers two full city blocks and boasts the highest elevator ride in the world. But it is first and foremost a serious work environment. Sears, however, no longer resides there, having relocated to the northwest suburbs in 1992. The Sears Tower continues to be both landmark and economic property, from which you can see five states on a clear day.

The skyline of Chicago continues to be dominated by the Sears Tower. Chicagoans take a special pride in the building's international reputation and its tourist draw. They relish the excitement this super-skyscraper continues to attract. The variety of its profile can be viewed from every angle and from the remarkable manner in which it presides within the context of the larger range of local manmade mountains.

Any discussion of the Sears Tower could easily center on the vast statistics of incredible proportions that intensify the superlative vocabulary that surround it—two million cubic square feet of concrete in its foundation, enough to build an eight-lane highway for five miles; or the supersonic speed of its elevators; or its 43,000 miles of phone cable; 2,000 miles of electric cable; 12,000 worker occupants; its 25,000 daily visitors or six robotic window washers. But in point of fact, the Sears Tower should be seen for what it is, a streamlined expression of beauty. A noble and majestic symbol of Chicago chutzpah. A brawny expression of Prairie attitude and the architectural proof that modernism can be elegant, efficient, and full of grace.

James R. Thompson Center

Architect: Helmut Jahn

Built: 1985

The local debate about the James R. Thompson Center is never ending. It is a subject on which there are no small opinions. Chicagoans either love it or hate it. Built as the State of Illinois' official office building in Chicago, at 100 West Randolph Street, it is named for former long-time Republican Governor James R. Thompson who originally commissioned Helmut Jahn to design the facility. Since it opened, in 1985, it has been a controversial structure, emblematic of Jahn who relishes his bad boy of architecture reputation.

Jahn and the Thompson Center are often referred to as "post modern," an architectural fine point that some dispute because they do not see a recognizable historical style reflected in his work. The building is best described as a large transparent dome, a sixteen-story, 160-foot rotun-

da, a 1.2 million square foot space under glass, which serves as the center of state government in Chicago.

The interior space is far more critical than the exterior in understanding this building. It is from here that you can see the skeleton of the structure. The inside of the dome is often an unsettling aesthetic experience. The intricate frame, formed of bright orange steel beams, is exposed and stands as an important part of

Right: Dubuffet's twenty-nine-foot tall black and white fiberglass monument outside the center.

Far Right: Helmut Jahn reinvented public space with the construction of Illinois' state office building in Chicago.

the ornamental embellishment, structurally and visually. Also exposed are the escalator gears and elevator mechanicals. Everything is part of the interior clockwork. In this government building, the architecture demands that everything be exposed.

Camera shops, dress shops, and candy stores are just some of the businesses that ring the lower floors, creating an indoor mall. Floors three to sixteen are occupied by the offices of state government. These office modules curve to fit the shape of the dome and are open to each other, and to the enormity of the dome's interior balcony-like lofts. Bright orange steel stairways create an architectural pattern which repeats the architect's maxim—if it is used, it should be seen. A lower concourse of 4,000 square feet is visible from the lobby through a seventy-two-foot diameter opening. Below, a variety of fast-food concessions make food available to lunchtime crowds.

Jahn not only exposes all the technology of the building, he displays all the workers and visitors as well within the glass elevators or throughout the open floors that encircle the public offices. When the building is crowded, the dome resembles the workings of a hive with human traffic and movement recreating the activity of bees. The glass skin permits a maximum of natural light to fill the interior space where everything is buzzing.

Externally, the immense, sloping glass façade of the building appears reminiscent of a spaceship. Its outer skin of bright silver, blue, and salmon color panels is Jahn's patriotic play on red,

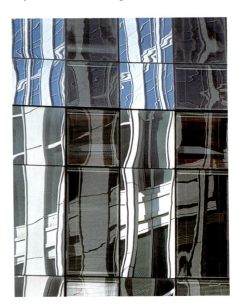

white, and blue. It is geometric and dramatic, but an architectural language that is difficult for many to understand.

The Thompson Center incorporates some remarkable streetscape elements that shape an open and unobstructed sense of public space. A public plaza has been created to enhance outdoor activity—lunchtime concerts, public rallies, political marches, and farmers' markets—the bread and circuses of Chicago life. The curving edge of the building's upper stories creates an overhang that canopies a section of the square and continues around the entire outside of the structure, providing important covering in inclement weather.

The Thompson Center represents an important redevelopment of a large area of the city's central business district. More than 3,000 men and women are employed within the arching dome. More than 1,000,000 square feet of it is utilized by government offices, with more than 150,000 square feet set aside for commercial use. All the train lines of the city's rapid transit system are accessible through the building.

Helmut Jahn has created an enormously complex piece of public space in the Thompson Center. It is often said that he is redefining what public space is all about in his design. But this bulky, bold, polychromatic dome says as much about the expectation of government as it does about how the public engages with, and uses, such space.

Above: The interior of the dome is a maze of labyrinthine passages.

Left: The reflective panels that create the skin of the Thompson Center are geometric and dramatic and resemble a spaceship at times.

Right: The red steel framing of the roof plane and dome wall.

Harold Washington Library

Architect: Hammond, Beeby, and Babka

Built: 1991 – 1992

The Harold Washington Library at 400 South State Street is a $130 million public building that makes Chicagoans proud. The massive red brick and granite flagship of the Chicago Public Library System is a dramatic, muscular monolith, an appropriate building of character to be the largest public library in the world. Named for the city's first African-American mayor, Harold Washington, during whose term of office the library's plans were begun, the building is the product of a dramatic architectural competition. A design jury of eleven members received the submission of five noted architectural firms who had accepted extensive guidelines for the design. Models were put on public display and the public had the opportunity to make their feelings on the designs known. The Chicago architectural firm of Hammond, Beeby, and Babka was selected for their submission of a ten-story postmodern building that many felt was "Sullivanesque."

The building bares the strong hand of its chief architect, Thomas Beeby. His design included thick granite walls, a red brick outer cladding, extensive external decorative embellishment and an extraordinary display of exaggerated and whimsical decorative metal roof sculptures and ornaments. The jury were

Right: Decorative ornamentation carries Chicago's motto, *Urbs in Horto*, City in a Garden.

Far Right: The dramatically massive postmodern design of the Harold Washington Library features extravagantly exotic owls perched on the roof.

Left: The library interior has been maximized for high use. Handsome interior woods create a pleasant environment.

Below Right: The exterior monastic motif is brought into the interior in these study carrels.

looking for a very particular architectural vocabulary and in this design they found it.

Beeby's library is ten-stories in height, one full city block square, and includes 750,000 square feet of space. He designed a true public building with mass and utility. His building sits on a rusticated granite base, horizontally framed with a decorative guilloche, an intertwining chain pattern set in stone. The granite is a reminder of Henry Ives Cobb's design at the Newberry Library and Louis Sullivan's frequent use of it in his robust designs. Nothing gives more size and strength to the exterior face than the soaring five-story vaulted window openings that vertically span several floors. They also express a dashing touch of the Romanesque flavor found at the Newberry, especially in the graduated arches of its triple entry wells. Here they achieve a monumental massing whose proportions set this structure apart from its neighbors, identifying it as a place of noble purpose.

The library is thick with exterior ornament. The façade is covered with stone iconography from themes of Chicago history. Above the main entrance on State Street, a twenty-foot ornamental horned owl sits nestled in a flowing bed of ebullient foliage. On each of the four corners of the building, a twelve-foot barn owl sits in similar botanical splendor. The owls are the work of sculptor Rau Kaskey of Washington, D.C. All are fabricated in aluminum and painted green to resemble weathered copper. Two other flowing metal sculptures, by artist Kent Bloomer, flow along the roof in rich designs of seedpods. They represent the classical tradition of ornamenting important buildings with botanicals. The building's top floor rises to a massive pediment on all four sides formed by wide glass curtain walls that are part of the library's interior winter garden. It prefigures the extraordinary mass of the full glass curtain that spans the west façade.

The interior of the library underscores the building's huge practical purpose. Floors three to nine contain the library's public holdings and educational and research infrastructure. Floors are arranged by topic and are uncluttered, spacious, and open. Light varieties of wood are used throughout in furniture, public counters, and interior paneling. An abundance of natural light brightens reading areas and shelves. Rich marbles and bronze terrazzo are used as well. More than 2,000,000 books are in circulation here, with more than seventy miles of shelves holding books for public use. The facility can accommodate 2,300 readers in countless niches and nooks that are bright and open, as well as extensive table space on every floor.

Beeby's postmodern design for the Harold Washington Library is rich in Beaux Art imagery and inspired by many classical touches from past vogues of Chicago architecture. However, the best feature of the structure's design success can only be identified by the public who use it. Beeby has created harmony and utility here, two indispensable elements in any public space. In a library, they are critical. Traffic flow, internal accessibility, elevator banks, and stairways are all important features for those using the building. So too is access to the collection. At the Harold Washington Library, Beeby's commitment to detail and function did not cease with the exterior grandeur, but rather continues within the user-friendly environment. Despite the massing and monumental scale of the building's proportions and artistry, this is also a gentle place, a beautiful place with respect for the people who use it. This dimension of its architectural character would bring wide delight to the famed Chicagoan for whom it is named.

UBS Tower

Architect: Lohan Caprile Goettsch

Built: 2001

The UBS (Union Bank of Switzerland) Tower at 1 North Wacker Drive, the corner of Madison and Wacker, was completed in 2001. Its sleek polish and gracious lines are still working on people. The fifty-story glass and steel high-rise did not sneak into the neighborhood. Instead, it has engaged it with dramatic dignity and surprising power. The cityscape, here, is electrified by its presence, its shimmer, its innovation, and its intriguing connection to people on the ground. What else could be expected from the first commercial high-rise in Chicago in the twenty-first century?

Lohan Caprile Goettsch, the Chicago architectural firm responsible for this fresh face in the skyline, debuted a building that is both bold and rational. It is innovative and thought provoking.

Pedestrians and tenants alike are immediately engaged at sea level by its beauty. Formed in a true Chicago-style, glass and steel construction, a form practically invented by partner Dirk Lohan's grandfather, Mies van der Rohe, the UBS Tower breaks away from the minimalism of the Chicago School while remaining reverential of its "less is more" philosophy. Chief architect James Goettsch fashioned a building of twenty-first-century

Left: Panorama of lobby viewed through ultra-transparent glass panels

Right: Sleek exterior skin of UBS Tower showing its east profile and the graduated setbacks that occur at the nineteenth and thirty-fourth floors.

technical utility beyond anything else in the city. Beneath the surface, the structure is a diamond mine of high-techno gadgetry and advanced telecommunication/internet shafts and cellular systems that are as flash-fast as the tower's high-speed elevators. At the same time, he has endeavored to make the first commercial high-rise to be constructed in a decade, something that will add texture and value to the architectural pantheon of Chicago life. In the twenty-first century, "aesthetics follow high-tech," it would appear. The tower has been called "a new brand of skyscraper," by *Chicago Tribune* architecture critic Blaire Kamin.

The building has great bones—linen finished stainless steel vertical bones to be precise, with silver-gray stainless panels along the horizontal spandrels and a glass skin of deep blue. Vertical stainless piers, visible on the north and south faces of the structure further define the tower's rolling, upward sweep. From these perspectives, the building sits within the lines of neighboring high-rises with a gracious sense of scale. It's not too tall. It's just right. This close to the Sears Tower anything else could be ludicrous. The UBS Tower, instead, acknowledges the grandeur and primacy of the Sears superstructure within its own graceful series of three setbacks along its eastern, Franklin Street, façade. Optically ogling UBS and the buildings just south of it from this Franklin Street panorama permits the viewer the best snapshot of Sears, from the northeast,

allowing its own progressive bundled setbacks to be seen almost side-by-side with those at UBS. It is a remarkable skyline-reflective tribute from the city's newest skyscraper to its tallest. UBS acknowledges its colossus down the street, but is unafraid of it architecturally.

Nothing is more architecturally dramatic to the eye at the UBS Tower than the lobby that sweeps across the width of one full city block, from Wacker Drive to Franklin Street. This oversized glass box with sleek stone

Right: Detail of window stabilizing pre-stressed cable roping and bronze medallion gear wheel.

Far Right: Exterior columns of burnished metal provide load bearing utility but also add dramatic beauty and fresh style.

surfaces and stainless steel columns pulls the ground traffic of pedestrians and workers into its sloping graded beauty. The forty-foot glass wall of windows here is the structure's signature architectural expression, its most memorable design characteristic that people easily engage with and then cannot stop talking about. These elaborate five-by-five foot panels of ultra-transparent glass are anchored by a pre-stressed steel cable rigging that resembles the roping on a schooner. Even in the "Windy City," it is said that this glass can withstand winds of up to 250mph. The surface reflectivity of this glass is so low that light is able to flood the interior even on overcast days. The revolutionary use of such innovative glass-wall construction is a reminder of the extraordinary use of glass by Daniel Burnham in the Reliance Building. Cladding on the massive lobby walls is a rich gray granite from India. An elipsing curve in the edge of the lobby's ceiling brings movement and simple beauty in high places.

Exterior landscaping is captivating and extensive—great stone dishes holding huge botanical balls from which trees lift up. They are strategically placed along the edge of the Madison Street curb, reconfiguring the heavy pedestrian traffic flow between the landscaping and the tower. Landscaping here shapes an urban garden for people to walk through, rather than serving as a botanical barrier between them and the building's façade.

Like all good Chicago architecture, the UBS Tower is about efficiency and practicality in the workplace. With 1,600,000 square feet of office space, the building's architectural features, like large structural bays, make flexible floor plates both efficient and necessary for the way people now work. But good Chicago architecture is also about the impact a structure adds by its presence. The Lyric Opera of Chicago, a UBS Tower across-the-street neighbor on Wacker Drive, is a grand dame of Art Deco classicism. Together they make a great mix, both aesthetically pleasing and well positioned. Opera-goers will undoubtedly find the smart new restaurant within the UBS Tower a welcome addition to the neighborhood. Its graceful utility is already making friends. Architectural beauty and good food—this is what Chicago loves.

Index